smart financial advice
for people on the way up

ready to be rich

Matt Reiner
creator of the benjamin™ bot

Printed in the United States of America

Library of Congress Control Number:
ISBN Paperback: 978-1-947368-93-4
ISBN eBook: 978-1-947368-92-7

Dedication:

To my wife, Hillary, who has made it possible for me to chase the wildest of dreams. And to everyone who has worked or interacted with Wela for helping me turn such a crazy idea into a reality.

Table of Contents

Acknowledgements:

This book would not be in your hands if it weren't for the tireless support of everyone in the Wela offices. The team at Wela have made Benjamin a reality that we are now able to share with the world. These extraordinary individuals have constantly pushed the envelope, and have bought into a vision that is changing people's lives. Each of them had a hand in making this book a reality, and every name listed here is as important as the one on the front cover, if not more: Hesom Parhizkar (Chief Technology Officer), James Hernandez (Lead Developer), Marisa Harris-Phang (Digital Content Producer), James Hart (Digital Video Editor), Justin Woods (Marketing Coordinator), Morgan Meyer (Associate Product Manager), Ethan Andrews (UI/UX Lead), Aura Jimenez (Administrative Assistant), Eddie Goepp (Chief Operating Officer, Client Strategist), Walt Coury (Client Strategist), and Tori Upshaw (Customer Success Manager).

The idea for this book came to me after I witnessed the success of my business partner and Wela co-founder Wes Moss in authoring and successfully launching *his* book. Wes had an integral part in guiding me through the process of writing a book that would engage readers and change lives. The time he was able to spend with me to help ideate, strategize, and ultimately execute is amazing.

To my other partners and co-founders at Wela, Mitchell and Michael Reiner, thank you. This book could not have been written without the support of everyone who has a hand in helping this company realize its vision.

Finally, the idea behind this book came from the innovation and growing open-mindedness that is beginning to emerge in the financial services world. This environment has allowed me to think outside the box about how we create a solid financial foundation for our clients while also allowing people to get what they want. Too often we are afraid of change, not because of the change itself, but because of the uncertainty that comes with having to deal with common situations in a different way. But when you are able to put yourself in an uncomfortable situation, some pretty amazing ideas can come out of it. I think that is what is happening in the financial services world, and that is what happened here with this book.

Chapter One

We Get It: Your Financial Life Is Really, Really Complicated

Finances. It's a word that most people dread, one that most people don't want to think about. It's not fun. It's not cool. It conjures up images of spreadsheets and calculators, of complex theories and complicated math. It evokes that creeping fear that we will not be able to provide for ourselves, for our family, for our future. It makes us imagine a life devoid of pleasure, a life of counting pennies just to ensure that we can survive the rest of our lives. If the word makes you break out in a cold sweat, you are not alone.

Humans are infinitely complex—but we are also very simple. We just want to do good, to provide for our families—and yet we also want to experience life. To many of us, saving means sitting at home, looking at the pictures our friends are posting of their amazing European vacations, and wishing we could do the same but knowing we can't because we have to save for our future. And it's no wonder that's the picture we have: so much of the financial advice currently available goes completely against the natural human instinct to enjoy life. But our lives are the sum of our experiences. If you're not living, if you're not experiencing things, if you're not enjoying life, then what's the point? Why count your pennies if you're not using them for anything?

If we can't plan our financial situation in a way that allows us to live life, then we are setting ourselves up for failure. So it's time to change the whole conversation. It's time to revolutionize the age-old concept of budgeting and financial planning that has clearly not been working for so many people.

Budgeting and financial planning don't have to be tied to doing and having less. With the right solution, you can actually live more, spend more, *and* save more. You just need the right philosophy, the right behavioral change—and that is what I'm hoping to show you in the following chapters.

I grew up in the financial-planning industry. I watched my dad build the wealth-management business he started twenty-five years ago. Focusing on individual families, my dad rethought the conversation when it came to income investing. I watched him help families transition from their working years to retirement while still being able to pass money on to their heirs.

Growing up in this environment, I always knew that I wanted to follow my father into the world of financial planning. Within three years of graduating from Arizona State, I studied for and obtained my Chartered Financial Analyst and Certified Financial Planner designations. I started working for my dad's business, where I still work today as a partner.

But as I worked there, as I was managing all of these individual families' investments—over $150 million, all told—I started to feel like I could do even more. I realized that I was really connecting with and relating to the people I was helping. I found that I was able to break down investing and explain it in such a way that we were able to truly understand one another, and I was therefore able to help these individuals create change in their own lives. There was nothing more inspiring than helping people transition from working to retirement, and then to have them come back to me and say, "Thank you. I've been traveling all over the world. I've been having the most amazing experiences that I never thought I would be able to afford, because of what you do."

As I approached my thirties, I started to watch my friends build their lives—getting married, buying houses. And my friends started coming to me for advice. That's when I realized that, just as my father had offered a change in the conversation for people getting ready to retire, I could work to offer a change in the conversation for people earlier in their lives, to help them understand how to get their financial affairs in order.

Out of that inspiration, nine years ago I cofounded Wela, a company at which I am the CEO. We started out as a traditional investment-management firm that focused on providing investment solutions for individuals who had under $500,000 in investable assets. Then, about four years ago, we decided we needed to do more. We went back to the drawing board with the aim of changing the way financial advice is delivered. We want to change the conversation, using technology to positively alter financial behaviors in a way that engages and liberates people rather than handcuffing them. We don't believe in planning out of fear; we believe in planning out of optimism and hope.

Now, I completely understand that having optimism and hope about your finances may seem like a fantasy. Your financial life likely feels far too complex and burdensome for you ever to be optimistic and hopeful about it. If you have a young family, you probably have a lot going on in your life. In a recent survey Wela completed of fifteen hundred individuals across the country, 73 percent of our married respondents have at least one kid—and 50 percent have two or more.

Kids are expensive! Additionally, the majority of our married respondents are employed—so not only are they dealing with kids, they are also dealing with work. Many young families also own houses or condos and have mortgages hanging over their heads. And that's not the only debt they are facing: many have student loans and/or credit card debt, too. Then, as their kids grow up, they have to think about the cost of education, from preschool—if they're thinking about private school—all the way through college, and potentially beyond. With all of those burdens, how the heck can anyone live a complete, satisfying life full of memorable experiences that bring joy and make life worth living?

Balancing a limited cash inflow with all those expenses and debts, *and* trying to save money—never mind finding some cash to actually have fun and meaningful life experiences—is a whole lot to have on your plate. And it can make thinking about the future pretty darn difficult. *I'm not worried about retirement,* we think. *I'm worried about paying off my credit card debt and my student loans. I'm worried about paying my bills this month. I'm worried about caring for my child. I'm worried about buying groceries this week. I'm not worried about my financial future because I'm just worried about making it through today.*

Over 60 percent of married individuals say they are worried about something in their financial future, such as being able to retire or paying off debt. However, when we asked those same individuals, "How do you feel about your financial future?" only 18 percent said they were either very or extremely worried. The majority responded, "I'm fine!"

As humans, we have an inability to comprehend a future that is unknown, despite the information and guidance we have in the present. So, even though we are kept up at night by financial worries, we also feel like everything will work itself out down the road. We are really good at avoiding issues, even though we know they exist. We think, *I'll just put off dealing with that until the future. I'll attend to it when things become a bit clearer, when I can wrap my head around it. Then I'll figure out how to make things better.*

When we are under all these financial stressors, it becomes incredibly difficult—even impossible—to make good financial decisions for our future. This is what gets us stuck in a rut, making decisions that continue to perpetuate the financial difficulties we're already facing instead of solving them. This isn't because we are failing somehow; it's actually a natural part of human psychology. In fact, this very phenomenon is central to the work of Daniel Kahneman and Amos Tversky, two psychologists who are considered the godfathers of behavioral economics. Kahneman won a Nobel Prize in economics in 2002, after Tversky passed away, and wrote a book called *Thinking, Fast and Slow*.

Kahneman and Tversky divide our thinking into two systems: System 1 and System 2. System 1 is fast, instinctive, emotional, and automatic. System 2 is the cognitive and rational part of our brain. It works more slowly, logically, and deliberately, not automatically.

We do not naturally, automatically use our System 2 brain. We have a limited amount of cognitive energy and effort that we can put into things. Therefore, we have to rely largely on our System 1 brain to get us through life. Some things we can transfer from our System 2 brain to our System 1 brain—driving, for example. When we first learn to drive, it requires a lot of conscious effort. But over time, while still requiring attention, it becomes instinctual and habitual.

When we overload our System 2 brain, we experience something called ego depletion. Psychologists did an experiment to illustrate this phenomenon. In the experiment, two groups of people were asked to memorize a set of numbers given to them by a scientist, then walk down the hall and repeat the set of numbers they were given to another scientist. The first group was given the numbers 2, 4, 6, 8, 10, and 12. The second group was given a random sequence of numbers.

As the people walked down the hallway to the second scientist, they were stopped by a third scientist who would say, "We thank you so much for participating in our experiment today, and we'd like to give you a little thank-you gift. You can have either chocolate cake or fruit salad. Which would you like?"

This question was the real experiment. The people given the even numbers mostly chose fruit salad, while those given the random numbers mostly chose the chocolate cake. Why? Because the people in the first group, with the even numbers, were mostly using System 1 to remember those numbers. Counting by twos comes pretty automatically to most people. So they had plenty of System 2 energy to think about which would be the healthier, better choice. The people who had the random numbers, on the other hand, were using a great deal of cognitive effort to remember their numbers. They were experiencing ego depletion. So their System 1 brain took over and made the easy, instant-gratification decision: chocolate cake.

If we are under financial stress, if we are putting constant System 2 effort into dealing with our financial situation, chances are that when it comes to making financial decisions, our System 1 brains will take over. We can't employ our cognitive skills to help us make smart choices. So we end up doing what is quick and easy, taking care of the immediate problems right in front of us rather than thinking through what will be better in the long term.

This certainly happens to me. I have a to-do list that I look at every day. Some tasks on the list are a lot easier than others, and I find myself always going toward the ones that are easier to knock out. It's a completely unconscious psychological tendency.

Without even thinking about it, I say, "This task's going to be difficult, I'm going to have to dedicate a lot of brainpower to it, so I'm going to get these other things done first." So I move that difficult task to the bottom of the list and put the smaller tasks at the top. Then, I end up spending my time on those smaller tasks and don't have time in the day to get to the harder tasks. So every night, I move that more difficult task to tomorrow's list. And the cycle repeats itself.

For most people—myself included!—big-picture financial planning feels way too huge to understand and way too huge to deal with on a day-to-day level—so we don't. We put it off. We place it at the bottom of our to-do list. *I'll deal with it all in one big chunk sometime down the road,* we think. *I'll meet with a financial advisor and take care of it all at once.* And then, when we're fifty-five or sixty years old and we need to get everything sorted out, we expect the financial advisor will wave a magic wand and everything will be all right. Unfortunately, financial advisors are not magicians, and that's not how finances work.

This practice of putting things off until later seems to be more and more the norm. Today, we generally have more debt and less saved for retirement—and less saved overall. A 2016 survey by the Federal Reserve Board found that 44 percent of respondents did not have the resources to cover a $400 emergency expense without borrowing money or selling something.[1] According to our own survey, 41 percent of married people don't even have $100,000 saved in investments or retirement. *It'll work itself out,* we think. *I'll be fine. It's far enough away that I'll just deal with it when I get there.* But when we get there, when we hit sixty years old and say, "I want to retire in ten years," we are

1. "Federal Reserve Board Issues Report on the Economic Well-Being of U.S. Households," Board of Governors of the Federal Reserve System, May 19, 2017, www.federalreserve.gov/newsevents/pressreleases/other20170519a.htm.

stuck. We haven't done any of the planning necessary to make retiring a possibility.

We avoid thinking about the future not only because it feels overwhelmingly complex, but also because it feels so very far away. If you're in your early to mid-thirties, like me, and you ask for financial advice, you'll likely hear the same thing over and over again: "Just save in your 401(k), and you'll be safe for retirement." This advice is absolutely true: you should save in your 401(k) for retirement. But let's be honest: With everything going on in our lives right now, how many of us are really going to be able to focus on something that won't happen for another thirty-five years? That is literally longer than I've lived! Am I really supposed to hop out of bed every morning saying, "I can't wait to save in my 401(k) today for something that is more than a lifetime away?"

A lot can happen in those thirty-five years. In your thirties, you have no idea what might happen between now and retirement. The idea of planning for all of those unknowns is completely overwhelming. *You're telling me to do something thirty-five years down the road,* we think. *How do I know where I'm going to be thirty-five years down the road? How do I know if I'm even going to* be *here thirty-five years down the road? I want to be able to live my life today, not just live for tomorrow.*

So much financial advice is focused only on the future—on making sure you're okay down the road. Its aim is to guarantee you can travel and enjoy life when you retire. That's all well and good, but what about today? I don't want to wait until I'm seventy to travel; I want to travel now!

I have good news: you can have your cake and eat it, too. You don't have to cut back your whole life just so you can finally enjoy life when you are seventy. You can keep living your day-to-day life while taking the necessary steps to ensure that you will be all set when you reach retirement. That's what we want to help you do. You just need to shift from *renting* your finances to *owning* your finances. Read on to find out what this means.

In our survey, we found that there are four fundamental things people want in their financial lives: to do good, to own a home, to get out of debt, and to enjoy experiences. Owning a home has long been a part of the American Dream, and our survey showed that that desire is still strong today across all ages and generations. People want to own a home because that means it's theirs. When you own a home, you control the outcome. You control what you do with the house, what modifications or repairs you make, what color it is, who maintains the lawn; everything about it belongs to you.

When you rent, all of that is controlled by someone else. You can still arrange the furniture how you like, you can still put pictures up on the walls, but you don't have the kind of control you do when you own. When you rent a house or an apartment, you are paying someone else. You don't own the appliances inside. You are not building equity. You don't have full control over when you'll have to move. You aren't settled.

Renting is not permanent. Everything is up in the air. Eventually, you will have to give it back. When you own a home, you know you don't have to give it back. It can't be taken away from you by a landlord. You can make it your own. It's a place to go that you know will always be there. It's permanent.

All of these differences between owning and renting a home can also be applied to your financial situation. Do you want to rent your financial situation, or do you want to own it?

The difference between owning and renting your finances is the difference between controlling your finances and letting your finances control you. If you are renting your financial situation, you aren't in control. If you own your financial situation, you have control over the situation. When you own a home, you have control over what happens to it. The same can be true of your finances. When you own your financial situation, you control your experiences, you control the outcome, you control the whole process—and you control where your money is going.

Renters are paying others as opposed to paying themselves. They aren't building equity via saving; they are simply maintaining what they have by paying out everything. When you rent your home, you are giving money to your landlord or management company every month. That money goes to somebody else. Month after month after month, you are giving away your money. When you own your home, even if you are paying off a mortgage, that money is going toward securing your future.

When you rent your finances, your money is going, going, gone . . . but it's not going toward you or your future. People who rent their financial situation don't know where their money is going. It's coming in the front door and going out the back door because they don't understand their finances.

When you own your finances, even as you spend money, you are also putting money toward your future—whether that's a vacation you are taking next year or your retirement down the road. Just as you would build equity in a house, when you own your finances, you are building equity into your future, into your financial goals and objectives.

Somebody who rents their finances is constantly worried about his or her finances and financial decisions. Renters are stressed day in and day out about whether they are going to be able to make next month's rent. They are constantly worried that everything is going to be taken away from them. Renters are the people who say, "I'm never going to be able to retire." They say, "I'm just doing this job to help me get by. But I can't afford to leave to look for a new job." They live paycheck to paycheck, wondering where all their money is going.

Financial renters are less likely to own their home. They don't have a documented budget, and they have less than $100,000 in retirement and investment savings. Renters are more focused on paying down debt and less focused on saving for retirement. They are not managing their debt effectively, and it is taking over their lives.

Those who own their finances understand and manage their budgets. They have either eliminated or are managing their debt very efficiently and effectively. They aren't letting their debt consume their whole financial situation. They are able to manage their debt while also managing their life experiences.

Owners are not worried about their financial future because they have such a good awareness and understanding of their financial situation. Renters, on the other hand, don't quite have that grasp. Renters lose track of what expected bills are upcoming, what money is in the bank, what they are trying to save for. They end up in a vicious cycle of never having enough money to do anything, with no idea how to get themselves out of the rut they are in. Renters are trapped by their financial situation because they can't get out of their own way. They are generally pessimistic about their financial situation because they don't understand what they need to do—and they don't think there's anything that they can do.

Owning your financial situation means understanding your financial situation. It means understanding what you need to do to continue to progress. It means having a clear vision and a clear path of where you need to go—so clear that you are able to make adjustments to add in vacations and other life experiences without worrying about your ability to move into the future.

Renters generally go on only one vacation a year and spend less than $1,000 on that vacation. Renters are stressed about their situation and can't let themselves spend money to create experiences. They are being held back by or are constantly battling their inability to experience and enjoy life today. They are more focused on ensuring that they can survive until tomorrow than on what they actually want to do tomorrow.

People who own their financial situation spend more money on things like vacations—not because they are making more money, but because they understand what they can do while still reaching their financial goals. Owners know how all the pieces fit together and integrate into one holistic situation and understand what they need to do to continue to propel themselves to the next level.

Renters are dreamers. Owners are doers. Owners take control of their financial situation in order to reach the goals they have for themselves, to actually live out their dreams. Owners are hopeful, aspirational, experiential. They are able to set and accomplish goals, to overcome financial hurdles, whereas renters are still trying to figure out and navigate their situation.

When you own your finances, it feels like a weight has been taken off your shoulders. You don't feel trapped or burdened by your financial situation, and that gives you the space to think more about what is really valuable in life. Owning your financial situation means it is under your control. You understand that you can both experience life and build wealth.

We want to help you move from being a renter to being an owner of your financial situation—and, once you are an owner, we want to help you stay there. Being an owner doesn't have any prerequisites. While many people who currently own their finances make over $100,000 a year, it is absolutely possible to own your finances even if you make less than that. You can have debt and still have a handle on your financial situation, just as you can make less than $100,000 and still be in control of your financial situation. It is possible to create a situation in which you are managing your debt, saving for retirement, and experiencing life today.

Of course, it will still take work. There is no such thing as waving a magic wand to eliminate of all your financial worries forever. I know that the very idea of dealing with your finances on a day-to-day level is completely exhausting. Who wants to think about budgeting and planning every single day? Navigating all of that feels so complex that many of us simply avoid it.

But it doesn't have to be overwhelming and complicated and impossible to understand. It can be simple. It can be practical. It can be done on a day-to-day basis without taking over your entire life. We want to show you how to streamline the complexity of your financial life into one simple action—an action that can help you better understand how today's decisions impact both your immediate future and your long-term goals.

You can get out of debt. You can care for your family. You can save for retirement. You can have a hopeful vision of the future, a future ripe with opportunity. *And* you can go on vacation. And you don't have to be a millionaire to do all this. It's not about money. It's about owning your finances instead of renting them, so that you can live your life today, full of experiences and enjoyment, while still achieving your dreams and goals in the future.

Chapter Two

Financial Planning Isn't Just for Rich Folks; It's for Regular Folks Who Wouldn't Mind Being Rich

The financial-planning industry has a stigma of being for the wealthy only. We all feel like the people we know who use financial planners are extremely rich. As someone who works in the financial-planning industry, I can tell you that there's some truth to this. There are even many financial-services companies that actually require a minimum net worth or investable assets in order to be a client. There's a patina of wealth that covers the world of financial planning, a feeling that because we're dealing with such important things, it has to be all mahogany desks and suits and ties. There's a sense that if you don't have shiny shoes, nobody will take you seriously as a financial planner. We're dealing with wealth, so we have to look the part.

But all of that fancy veneer paints an exclusionary picture: it makes non-wealthy people think, *I'm not worthy of that. I'm not worthy enough—not wealthy enough—to go and talk to those people. My clothes aren't that expensive. My shoes aren't that shiny. They're going to look at me and laugh.* Who wants to ride the elevator to the twenty-fifth floor of a tall building, sit across a mahogany desk from someone with shiny shoes, and be told, "You are spending too much. You're never going to be able to retire. You've got way too much credit card debt. Also, by the way, if you have anybody that you can refer to me, please send him my way, I'd like to chat with him." Nobody wants to listen to that. We just want a plan. We just want to learn what to do and how to do it—and not be judged in the process.

Many people feel like they don't know enough to talk to a financial advisor. You have a limited amount of time with this professional, and you don't even know what questions to ask to get you where you want to go. You don't want to ask the wrong question because you want to make the most of that limited time. But you don't have enough information or knowledge to know what the wrong questions are. So it feels like it would just be a waste of time and money to meet with one. Why would you put yourself in that situation?

We all get embarrassed when we lack knowledge, especially when we're talking to a professional. And the financial professionals don't always help. All too often, they actually make things seem even more complex than they really are, and impossible to implement without constant hands-on advice—and who can afford that? Moreover, you're always worried that they're going to sell you something, taking advantage of the fact that you don't fully understand the ins and outs of financial planning. *Are they going to try to sell me life insurance?* you wonder. *Disability insurance? Are they going to throw me into this high-cost mutual fund? I don't even really know what a mutual fund is!*

Even if you do feel like you have a grasp on the concepts of financial planning, the idea of going to a financial advisor can feel like going to the dentist. I hate going to the dentist because I always feel like he's judging me for not flossing enough or not brushing my teeth correctly. I know I need to floss more; I just hate him telling me so!

People feel the same way about going to a financial advisor—except even more so, because it's their money, their livelihood, their life. We avoid dealing with our finances because many of us are afraid that we will fail—that we won't stick to our budget, that we won't save enough, that we have already done so poorly that we are now a completely lost cause. We don't want to know if that's true—and, even more, we don't want anybody else to know. We can't bear the prospect of facing that shame, so we just avoid it.

As humans, we don't like being judged. Your financial situation is incredibly personal and revealing the details of it to someone can make you feel very vulnerable. That's why we tend to keep information about our money, income, and spending habits to ourselves. We don't share it with our friends or neighbors or even our family.

We get embarrassed about our financial situation because we think everybody else has it more together than we do. But that's not at all true; it's just that we don't talk about it. Society tells us to keep all of that to ourselves. What if we could all just be open and accepting about dealing with our finances? What if we could get rid of the shame and embarrassment? It would be so much easier to admit to ourselves that we could use help, to seek it out, to hold ourselves accountable, if we didn't feel like we would be judged for doing so. But instead, we say—to other people and to ourselves, "Yeah, I'm just researching which options are right for me. I'm working on it. I'm fine; I just haven't had the time to figure it all out yet."

The truth is, if you actually did put it out there, nobody would care. People are not going to judge you because we are all in the same boat! We all mess up, we all need help, and none of us has it all worked out perfectly. It's easy to think that your financial situation is so messed up that a financial advisor is just going to shake his or her head and walk away. Here's the secret: everyone's financial situation is messed up in one way or another. However out of whack you think your finances are, I guarantee you that they look a lot like a lot of other people's finances, so you don't need to feel ashamed or embarrassed.

When I was at my father's company, I had clients who would come in with $300,000 or $400,000 and say to me, "I'm never going to be able to retire." In their minds, they had to have a million dollars or more in order to retire, because that's what they thought other people were doing. I would have to break down for them how, in fact, they could absolutely retire on what they had—and have a full and vibrant retirement, too! It was just a matter of reorganizing their thinking so they could stop comparing themselves to others and instead live full lives based on their own situation.

We all compare ourselves to our neighbors, but because it's considered uncouth to talk about money, we don't actually know what we are comparing ourselves to. We see our friends posting on social media and we make assumptions based on what we see. If we see friends posting about their amazing vacation, we assume that they must have more money than us since they're able to afford that trip. And that makes us feel like we are poor—or, at least, poorer than our friends.

That *may* be true, but it may not be. We can't base our own financial decisions on how much money we assume other people have. If you feel like you don't have any money, you will live your life like you don't have any money. When you feel like you are not making enough money, it's very easy to say, "I can't do anything because I have no money." That's the easy, System 1 conclusion our brain comes to: "There's nothing I can do."

By showing you how you can spend more and save more—by showing you how you can own your finances instead of renting them—financial planning can help you stop feeling like you're poor so you can stop living like you're poor. It can help you overcome the hurdles that paralyze people until it's too late. But it is also difficult. It's burdensome. Nobody should be expected to do it on his or her own! Everybody needs help and guidance—or at the very least, moral support, because there are going to be bumps in the road, and when they appear, we all need help to stay motivated, to not just give up.

Unfortunately, there are many financial advisors out there who will say, "If you only have $25,000, then all you can do is spend nothing." And what they are really thinking is, *Get this person out of my office so I can focus on my million-dollar client.* Spending nothing is the easy answer and, sadly, it's the one many advisors reach for first. The financial-planning industry has been saturated with salespeople who are just selling for their own profit, as opposed to working for the benefit of the individual.

The fact that financial services are generally geared toward the ultra-wealthy is built into the history of the financial-planning industry. In the 1800s, only the really, really rich could afford to buy and sell stocks. This remained true for nearly a century. Goldman Sachs, Bear Stearns, JPMorgan, Merrill Lynch, Morgan Stanley—all of these firms really only catered to the wealthy. It was not until the mid-1970s that Charles Schwab and Vanguard brought a discount-brokerage model to the table, opening the door for another, less wealthy set of individuals to buy, sell and invest.

In the 1990s, E*Trade, Scottrade, and other e-investment platforms came along, which allowed the do-it-yourselfers to invest without ever dealing with a broker. In 2009, Betterment and Wealthfront started offering services that buy and sell for you, so you can invest without even worrying about buying and selling. The pie has now been expanded so just about anybody can afford to invest.

But that hasn't solved the true problem. A person can't go to Betterment and say, "I need help planning my finances. I want to better my financial situation. What do I do?" Betterment can't give you that advice. They may tell you to continue using them to invest, but that's about it. They aren't going to take the time to get to know you, to understand all aspects of your financial life. They aren't going to help you get your financial affairs in order.

Many people see the words *financial planning* and think they only mean buying and selling stocks or investments. *That doesn't help me,* they think. *I need to figure out things like how to pay my bills every month, live my life, and plan for the future at the same time.* And so, naturally, they conclude that financial planning is not for them.

And in some ways, they're right. Many financial-planning services—especially those not geared toward the uber-wealthy—simply offer tools for investment management. They don't actually deliver holistic financial advice. A Merrill Lynch or Morgan Stanley advisor would be great at helping you plan your investments, but they're not going to help you identify how to break down your spending habits to increase your savings. That just doesn't happen; it's not the expertise they have. The financial-planning industry is focused on revenue and profits—just like every industry is. It's focused on getting you to invest. It's not focused on holistic planning.

Though the financial-planning industry has been in existence since the 1800s, we still haven't solved the problem of giving holistic financial advice to individuals without a high net worth. The irony is that such people are often the ones most in need of financial-planning assistance. If you are wealthy, you can afford to make mistakes. Those of us who are not super wealthy can't afford to make big mistakes—but there's no one out there helping us to avoid them.

Young, non-wealthy families as a demographic are largely neglected by the financial-services industry when they are, in fact, the people who probably need it the most, as they juggle bills and debt and kids and trying to make ends meet. In the model we currently have, who is going to help ordinary people get rich, as opposed to helping people who are already rich stay rich? Both are needed, but the former group gets completely neglected.

We need solutions that work for the non-millionaires, that help us regular folks tackle the financial issues we have today. We need financial planning for you and me. The problem is, financial planning advice hasn't changed in—well, pretty much ever. "Save more; spend less." "Save for big things." "Spend less than you make." "Put money in your 401(k)." If you Google "financial advice for a young professional," you'll see all of this same advice repeated over and over again.

Now, all of that advice still holds true. The problem is that the way we deliver and implement this advice also has not changed—and it clearly isn't working for a whole lot of people. Over 70 percent of the individuals in our survey who are making less than $100,000 a year have less than $100,000 in savings. And over 50 percent of those individuals are forty-five years old or older. But getting to $100,000 in savings by the age of forty-five shouldn't be a difficult task. It just takes the right strategy to get there—and there are far too few financial-planning services out there to help you figure out what that strategy is.

You may be wondering what secret advice rich people are getting from financial advisors that seems to work so well for them. In fact, wealthy people are given the exact same advice: save more, spend less than you make, and pay off your debt by the time you retire. The difference is, when you have more money, everything moves faster, with bigger results. Take compounding, one of the cornerstones of financial planning. The higher the amount you start with, the more money you're going to have at the end. Growing $100 or $1,000 by 10 percent a year doesn't yield all that much—only $10 or $100 a year, respectively. Even if it's $10,000, at the end of the year, 10 percent growth will only get you $1,000. But if you're a millionaire and you grow a million dollars by 10 percent—well, that's $100,000. That's a lot of money right there.

Even though it's the same percentage return—10 percent—our minds think in nominal (dollar) values, not percentages. Of course, $100,000 is much bigger than $10,000, even though they are both a 10 percent gain. Our motivation is based on how we interpret things, and we interpret progress and gaining wealth in dollars, not percentages.

So, if you are seeing your money grow by $100,000 a year, that's some major motivation. It really feels like you're getting somewhere. If, on the other hand, you are only seeing your money grow at $100 or $1,000 a year, it's difficult to imagine that you will ever reach $100,000. It's not easy to stay motivated to stick with your plan. Feeling like you're ever going to achieve your goals is near impossible. It's hard to see why you should bother.

Moreover, when you're a millionaire, it's easier to put money away and forget about it. You have enough to rely on for your day-to-day life. If you're working hard to make ends meet, putting aside a thousand dollars to accrue interest may seem impossible. It's difficult to create a habit of putting away money when you feel like you need every dollar to get through the month.

So many of the messages and advertisements we see from the financial-planning industry proclaim their ability to help you retire with millions. A few years ago, ING ran a series of commercials that asked, "What's your number?" The commercials showed people walking around with a number floating over their head, which was meant to represent the amount of money they would need to retire. Pretty much all of the numbers the commercials showed were above a million dollars.

I don't know about you, but as soon as I see something talking about millions of dollars, I think, *Well, that's clearly not intended for me. It doesn't apply to me at all.* And I stop paying attention. It feels so far outside the realm of possibility that we figure the whole industry must not be for people like us. We're never going to have millions when we retire, so why shouldn't we just keep living our lives and not bother with that whole financial-planning thing?

Traditional financial advice says that in retirement, you need 80 percent of your current income. If you're making $60,000 a year, that math adds up to needing over a million dollars to retire. Most of us look at that and say, "Well, great. I'm never going to get there. So I guess I'll never retire. I'll just work for the rest of my life." And if you're in your fifties, say, and barely have anything saved for retirement, you're probably even more discouraged by all these messages about saving millions. You especially may feel like there's no point in even trying because it's too late; you'll just have to work forever and live off instant ramen for the rest of your life.

Those feelings are understandable, but they're not based in reality. You can still retire. It'll take some work, but don't think about all of a sudden having to come up with a million dollars in the next ten years. Start with smaller increments. When someone says, "Go save a million dollars," a person who is only making $50,000 a year is going to think, *There's no way I'm going to get there.* But the truth is, you can get there—if you don't try to go out and save a million dollars. Don't focus on millions. Instead, focus on that first $100,000.

We hear wealthy, successful people say, "The first million is the hardest," or, "The first billion is the hardest." Well, sure—the first million seems nigh impossible, in fact. A million doesn't even seem like a real number. I don't understand what that number means. It's impossible to try to achieve something that I can't even wrap my mind around. But I can wrap my mind around $1,000, $10,000, even $100,000. Now, the same holds true for the first $100,000 as for the first million: the first $100,000 is also the hardest. It's going to take the most effort, the most work. The next $100,000 is much easier, and the next $100,000 even easier.

The trick is to work in stages. Don't try to plan how you're going to save a million dollars, or $100,000, right now. When you look back at your life, it is the small milestones that got you where you are today, the accumulation of all those small steps. The same is true for saving. Imagine playing a video game that has no checkpoints, no levels. You just have to play the whole thing all in one go. No one would play that game, right? What keeps us playing is the fact that we can just beat one level at a time. We can focus on the level we're on, then, once we beat it, we move on to the next level, and then the next, until finally we beat the whole game.

Moreover, each checkpoint gives us a progress point. If we fail at one level, we don't go all the way back to the beginning. We get to start at our last checkpoint and keep moving forward instead of sliding all the way back to where we started. Each checkpoint is a stepping-stone that progresses us further. And each time we beat one of those levels and reach a new checkpoint, we feel like we've really accomplished something, which keeps us motivated. That's what keeps us playing.

Why can't we do the same thing with financial information and financial advice? When all of the advice is, "You need millions of dollars to retire," it's like playing the whole game all at once. Instead, we need to ask, "How can we get that first $10,000 in savings?" We can strategize and plan to reach that goal because it is actually imaginable. It is actually achievable. Focusing on that huge end goal is completely overwhelming. Instead, focus on the shorter-term goals. And I will tell you that if you do that, you will look back forty years down the road and be amazed at what you have achieved.

You just need a plan—and you just need to stick to it, because these things do take time. It takes time to pay off debt. It takes time to grow wealth. There's no silver bullet for that. But as is true with a fine wine, all good things come in time. You just need to believe in the plan and believe in the process.

The problem is, the long term is the only thing traditional financial planning focuses on. There's no advice on how to engage more in the world today while still taking these steps to plan for your future. In our survey, we found that people making under $100,000 a year were much more worried about their debt situation, about their retirement, about paying their bills each month. They are focused on and stressed about day-to-day issues. They feel like they can't do anything more than just try to take care of those concerns. What's the point of having your future all set if you have no idea how you're going to survive and live your life until then?

We don't need to change the advice; we need to change how it is delivered. All of this advice is delivered as is—bits and pieces of financial wisdom—but nobody explains how to actually implement these things. The advice is broad and general. It's correct, but it is incredibly difficult to understand how to apply it practically. Nobody provides any specifics. When we get this advice, we still have to digest it and understand it. What does it mean to me? How does it relate to me? How does it impact me? How do I apply this advice based on my own personal situation?

In general, financial people are very analytical, very numerical. *One plus one equals two,* they think. *There's no way that one plus one could ever equal three, so I'm not even going to think about it. There's one way to do this because it's simple math.* Of course, math is math; it's not going to change. But what we can change is the way the information is implemented. We can use that information in a more helpful way that can actually make a change in your day-to-day life. We can offer advice that allows you to develop financial habits, habits that benefit you both in the short term and in the long term. We can offer a new approach for those who are all but left behind in today's financial-services world—an approach that will help you move from renting your finances to owning your finances.

Chapter Three

Let's Tell the Truth: Budgeting Sucks

Just like financial advice in general, budgeting hasn't changed in centuries—and, clearly, it is not working. Many people don't have a budget at all; according to our survey, 64 percent of people making under $100,000 a year in household income do not have a budget in place. And many of those who do have a budget are still worried about their financial situation. In our survey, 53 percent of people with a budget have less than $100,000 saved. What is going on? Why, if they have a budget, are they not able to save anything? Where is that money going? Why are people with budgets still renting their finances instead of owning them?

It is clear that our current model of budgeting is not creating better spending and saving habits. It's often said that the definition of insanity is doing the same thing over and over again and expecting a different result. We've been doing budgets the same way for centuries and we are not getting different results. Nothing has changed. People aren't getting any better at it. Instead, their financial situations continue to get worse. Fewer and fewer people are budgeting, even though there are more and more budgeting tools available. We are not getting to the root of the problem.

Older generations say, "This generation doesn't know how to budget. They don't know how to manage their finances." But we're not giving them any new tools that they can actually understand and use. We're just giving them the same tools *we* used. If we all thought and did the same as the generation before us, we wouldn't advance at all. We wouldn't have cars. We wouldn't have cell phones. We wouldn't have email. We would still be riding in horse-drawn buggies.

Everything else changes from generation to generation. Why hasn't budgeting? Traditionalists say, "Because it's math. It's numbers. One plus one always equals two." And that's true; the basic principles of budgeting will never change. But the approach and the process *can* change. Babies are still born in the same way they have always been (in most cases), but the process and approach have changed dramatically over time. Why can't the process and approach to budgeting change as well?

The budgeting conversation has always centered on numbers rather than behavior. We need to change the conversation, getting away from numbers and focusing instead on how we can help people change their behavior to help them stick to their plans. We need to revolutionize our way of thinking about budgeting.

The idea behind budgeting—tracking your money so that you know how much to save and spend—is obviously an essential one. But the way we have been going about it for centuries clearly doesn't work for a lot of people. Budgeting advice tends to be one-size-fits-all. It doesn't take into account how differently people live their lives, or what different people want to spend money on that creates value in their lives.

The budgeting advice we've been given for centuries looks something like this: Create a spreadsheet. Categorize your spending and track it. Save your receipts. Track your credit card bill and bank accounts. Remember to maintain that spreadsheet and revise it every month, or even every week; otherwise, it all goes to hell.

The tools to do this have evolved over time. In the past, budgeting had to be done with a pencil and paper (and some people still prefer that method); now it can be done in an Excel spreadsheet. Today there are apps, such as Mint, that help you track your expenses. They may even help you set goals and plan for the future. But ultimately, the burden of doing the work still falls on you. You still have to go through and aggregate all the information from your various financial institutions. You still have to track everything, try to predict your spending, and enter all those numbers into the spreadsheet or into a particular app. You still have to put in the work to categorize everything. You still have to make sure everything's assigned to the right column. You still have to set your amounts and limits.

With every single transaction, every time you spend money, you have to determine which category it fits into and calculate how it plays into your budget. Every time you buy something on Amazon, you have to figure out whether it belongs in entertainment or travel or food or stuff for your kid—and which category of stuff for your kid?

Our brains aren't meant to calculate numbers on the fly all the time. The average person—no matter how smart or how good at math he or she is—isn't going to be able to keep track of every category and expense and add it all up and factor it all in every single moment, every single day. People don't want to have to think about their budget all the time. I certainly don't! It takes so much time and effort. It's a huge mental burden. Maintaining a budget becomes a chore, rather than an exercise that helps you progress toward the things you want. Even with today's technology, it's time consuming and unrewarding.

Nearly 60 percent of people who have a budget and make less than $100,000 a year look at their budget either weekly or daily. Nobody wants to spend thirty minutes or an hour every week sitting at the kitchen table maintaining his or her budget. That's not normal for your everyday life. It feels punishing. Every time you mess up and go over budget, you have to do more work, but there's no equivalent reward when you *don't* mess up.

This kind of budgeting really only gives you two options: you either have to pull out your spreadsheet and do complicated math every time you want to spend money, or you say, "It's too much," and you abandon your budget—and get in trouble further down the road. Often, people build these complex budgets, stick to them for three months, and then give up. It's just too difficult. It doesn't seem worth it. And unless you are a very numbers-oriented person who can focus on the smallest and finest points, you are not going to be able to stick to your budget for a long period of time. If you have to deal with it every single week, every single month, you're never going to stick to it. That's far too much work.

Moreover, no matter how careful you are, something is always going to come along that throws things off. In our survey, 75 percent of people said the biggest reason they don't stick to a budget is because of life getting in the way. Sometimes life just happens. Your car gets sideswiped on the street and you have to bring it in for repair. Your kid gets sick and you have to stay home from work or pay for a babysitter. You cut your hand while cooking and need to get stitches. Or maybe your friend gets engaged and invites everybody out to a fancy dinner to celebrate, and you spend a hundred dollars you didn't plan on spending. All of a sudden, your budget is completely out of whack. Your spreadsheet's in ruins and Mint is telling you how completely you screwed up. After all that work, after all those careful calculations, how the hell are you supposed to get back on track?

Traditional budgeting says that the way to deal with life getting in the way is to have an emergency reserve. That means budgeting appropriately over time to build up that emergency reserve, determining how much should be kept in it and figuring out how to replenish your emergency reserve when you need to dip into it—never mind how to manage if multiple life events happen one after the other.

Sounds impossible, right? It's no wonder that most people don't even bother. Even though everyone is told that they need to have an emergency reserve, very few people do. Instead, they'll put things on their credit cards, building up debt while only paying their minimum. Their credit card debt builds up, and within a year their debt is out of control. Life got in the way and they didn't have an effective plan to adjust their budget and get things back under control after that unexpected life event.

When life gets in the way, traditional budgeting makes you say, "We can't spend money because we already spent it on this life event." It tells you that you have to cut back on everything in order to pay yourself back for the money you spent. It makes you feel like you have to bring your life to a screeching halt just because an unexpected life event happened.

Even *expected* events can throw things out of whack. It's Christmas. Then it's your kid's birthday. Then it's your anniversary. And then you're so off track that it seems pointless to try to get back on track. You can't see how you can ever get better because you keep blowing out your food or entertainment budget and you run out of wiggle room.

When you have one or two bad months, you think, "Well, this is never going to work." And you give up. It seems too difficult to get back on track.

People hate budgeting because they feel like they're setting themselves up for failure. They know they're not going to stick to it, so they avoid doing it because they want to avoid feeling bad. So they kick the can down the road. *I'll start budgeting when I have a kid,* they think. Then they have a kid and they think, *I'll start budgeting when I need to start saving for the kid's college.* And they keep kicking it down the road.

Instead of budgeting, some people figure they can just keep track of things in their head, using mental accounting. People think that if they know more or less how much they have coming in and going out, they don't need a budget. But if you're budgeting in your head, you may well be missing out on the bigger picture.

Richard Thaler, who recently won the Nobel Prize in economics, is well known for his work on mental accounting. He conducted a study on taxi drivers in New York City—before Uber or Lyft existed—to determine how long they would work each day based on the weather. Would drivers work more hours on rainy days or on sunny days?

Intuitively, you would think that drivers would work more on rainy days because more people use taxis on rainy days. Surprisingly, Thaler found the opposite. Taxi drivers would actually work longer on sunny days.

Why? Because the drivers had set daily earnings objectives for themselves. On a rainy day, when everybody wants a ride, they would hit that goal within a short amount of time, and then they would go home. On sunny days, they might drive around all day and never hit that number.

Having daily earnings objectives sounds like a pretty good system, right? Easy to keep track of on a day-to-day basis, easy to keep track of in your head. But when you look at the bigger picture—not at just one day, but at a week, or a month, or a year—you reach a very different conclusion: if the taxi drivers worked longer hours on rainy days and shorter hours on sunny days, they would actually make more money.

If you focus on a narrow framework, it may lead you to do something that makes sense today, but that is actually completely nonsensical from a longer-term economic perspective. That's why you need a budget that accounts for the bigger picture—because the bigger picture is the whole point. The goal of a budget is simple: to get you to spend less than you make and still allow you enough to both cover your current expenses and save toward your future financial goals. The problem is that we are conditioned to come at it backwards. The question should not be, "Do you have a budget?" The question should be, "Do you have a plan?"

A budget by itself—what good is that? You're spending less than you're making, you're spending within your limits, but what are you working toward?

The truth is, a budget is just a tool. It's not the end; it's the means to the end, which is a financial plan. A financial plan provides the bigger picture of your financial life, from vacations and big investments, like buying a house, to how to pay for your kid's college, to how much you need to save to retire. A financial plan is what allows you to own your finances. The budget is the tool to help you achieve your plan.

A plan is hopeful. A plan says, "This is what I can do. These are things that I want to accomplish." A plan is a visualization of the good things that are going to happen in the future. If your only plan is to get out of debt, it may be nothing more than budgeting—saving and cutting costs just to pay off your debts. But your plan doesn't have to be the same as your budget. Instead, you can *start* with a plan. Start with hope, with the happy place where you want to be. Then you can use your budget to help you get there.

Too often we say, "OK, let's figure out our budget, and then we'll figure out what we can afford to do." Instead, we should be saying, "Let's figure out what we want to do, and then let's figure out how to get there." Starting with a budget is renting your finances. Starting with a plan leads to owning your finances. Start with your plan and work backward from there. A budget should help you understand how your everyday spending decisions are affecting your ability to progress toward the plan you desire. Let your plan drive your budget, rather than the other way around. Let your hopes and goals drive you, rather than limits and rules.

Even if you're really good at budgeting and staying within your limits, you should be working toward something—something that should guide your plan. Perhaps you want to advance your career by going back to school; if so, your plan should reflect that. Maybe you're going to move to a new city to pursue a new opportunity; your plan should reflect that as well. And all the while you should still be able to save for retirement, build up emergency reserves, and pay down credit card debt, no matter what your income is.

Interestingly, one of the responses to our survey question about why people don't make budgets was "not enough money." People think that if they had more money, they would be able to stick to a budget better. They think that life wouldn't get in the way, and that their lack of discipline wouldn't be as problematic because they'd have the money to cushion themselves.

That's actually not how it works at all. Having more money doesn't solve the problems of discipline, time and effort, or life getting in the way. If you have more money, your lack of discipline will just enable you to make bigger mistakes, which will hurt just as much. Life problems that get in the way just become bigger life problems that cost more money because you are putting yourself in different positions—for example, buying a more expensive car that costs more to repair if it is damaged. People think that if they have more money and buy more things, their problems are going to go away—but really, you just have more complex problems.

Moreover, simply having more money is not going to help you get where you want to be. Having more money does not mean that you own your finances. You still need a plan. And no matter what your income is, your budget should be the day-to-day, month-to-month guiding tool that allows you to achieve that plan. Your budget should be a tool to build your financial castle rather than a weight keeping you from reaching your financial objectives. You need a plan that gives you the "why" behind your current budget, and that allows you to have some ownership over the development of the budget.

Of course, if you're spending three hours a week on your budget, your budget is naturally going to feel like the most important thing. You're spending all your time on it; how are you supposed to focus on a plan? But if your budget can be simplified and streamlined so that you can stick to it without it taking over your life, then your plan will become the bigger and more important thing. You can focus on the plan instead of the budget.

Unfortunately, all the tools and applications and processes we've come up with have only succeeded in making budgeting more complex. There is so much information we have to contend with that we get overwhelmed and end up paralyzed.

In every area of life, we think that the more tools we have, the easier things will be. When I walk into The Container Store, I think, "Oh man, if I just owned everything in this store, my life would be so organized. If I had all those drawers, my house would be a paragon of organization. I would know exactly where everything is." But when I actually try to do that—when I put in all these drawers—all of a sudden, I have no idea where anything is. It's too complicated. I have no idea which drawers I've put certain things into, and I don't know where to find anything. It's completely overwhelming.

The same is true of budgeting. If we just keep throwing tools at people, they just become overwhelmed with tools. Now they have fourteen different apps and programs to try to maintain one budget—and thirty categories of expenses to keep track of.

You don't need more drawers or more apps or more categories; you need a simpler process. What if, instead of creating complicated systems, we focused on changing financial behavior? What if, instead of creating more and more tools, we actually focused on the underlying roots of our problems?

Does it really matter how much I spend on entertainment versus food versus travel? Do we really have to put all that time and effort into determining whether something is a food expense or an entertainment expense or a travel expense? Is that really helping us manage our budgets? Why can't we streamline the whole process? Let's make fewer hurdles for you to jump through to stick to your budget, rather than more. Why do I need to spend three hours every weekend combing through my budget and calculating categories to see where I stand? What if, instead of spending three hours every Sunday working on my budget, I could do it in two minutes while I'm brushing my teeth—and then have those hours free to spend with my family or friends?

We need to simplify the whole thing. Our ability to adopt a habit, behavior or tactic depends on three things: it's got to be easy; it's got to be normal; and it's got to be rewarding.

If we have to overcome the hurdle of learning to understand something complicated, we are more likely to avoid it. If something is easy to understand, it is easy to implement in our lives. It also has to be normal, so that it fits into our everyday life. If it's complicated and exhausting to maintain, if it takes you away and detracts from your everyday life, then you are never going to stick to it.

And if we are going to stick with something, it also has to be rewarding in some way. It's hard to stay motivated if there are no rewards for your hard work. It's not easy to stay on track when your only reward is coming thirty years down the road, when you retire. We need to feel a sense of internal satisfaction, not just in the long term, but in the short term as well.

Most financial-planning and budgeting tools are complicated and difficult, certainly don't fit into an everyday routine, and often feel like a punishment. When you hear the word *budget*, I bet you hear the same thing I do: "Don't spend, don't spend, don't spend." For centuries, budgets have always said one thing: "Don't do that." Budget means limits. It means not spending money. A budget is something that tells you, "No."

Nobody likes to be told no, to be told not to do something. Most of the time, it just makes us want to do that thing even more! If all you're hearing is, "Don't spend this. Limit yourself on food. Limit yourself on entertainment. Limit, limit, limit," at some point you're bound to say, "Well, screw this."

People think of things as being either black or white. You can spend or you can't spend. You can go on vacation or you can't go on vacation. If you want to get out of debt, you have to do this, that, and the other. You start thinking that you have to get rid of every little thing. *I guess I can never take a vacation again,* you think. *I guess I can never eat out. I guess I should cancel my Netflix subscription.* It starts affecting how you live your day-to-day life because you feel like you have to stop doing everything in order to stick to your budget. You start cutting things—and yet it doesn't make a difference because you haven't actually figured out how those expenses work with everything else.

But it doesn't have to be that way. It doesn't have to be black or white. If you integrate everything into a comprehensive plan, you can actually spend *and* save. We need to step back and analyze how we've been promoting budgeting. We need to see whether there's another way we can communicate. We need to change the language from, "No, you can't spend," to, "Yes, you can improve your financial situation."

For far too long, we've been saying that the problem is with the person, not the process. "If you can't change as a person in order to stick to your budget," the thinking goes, "then we can't help you." What we should be asking is, "How can budgeting put you in a better position to succeed?" We should be figuring out how to change the process to better fit the person, so the person can be more successful.

If we really want people to get better financially, to own their finances, to be able to plan for themselves and their families—to budget—then we need to have a simple process. You need something that will grow and evolve as you grow and evolve, without becoming more complex. No matter what stage of life you are at, it should remain just as simple, and you should be able to continue using it the same way. You need a process that says, "Yes, you *can* do things." Life shouldn't get in the way of your budget; your budget should help you create the life you've always wanted.

We have a budgeting tool that we believe will help you do all these things. It's called the Daily Spend Limit.

Chapter Four

Introducing the Daily Spend Limit

The Daily Spend Limit is a budgeting solution that encompasses all of the aspects of a great budget that we've identified. We aren't finding a loophole in the system to help you find money easier and faster; rather, we've identified a way to help each of us overcome the psychological barriers that stop us from sticking to a budget and changing our relationship with our finances.

In order for the Daily Spend Limit to work, you have to use it. It's a tool, and if you don't use the tools you have, you're never going to build anything. As with any other type of budget, you have to stick to it in order for it to work.

But beyond that, the Daily Spend Limit isn't like other budgeting tools—the ones that don't work, the ones that suck. It's a tool that makes the work easier. Imagine that you're putting a piece of furniture together and all you have is a screwdriver. People keep handing you new screwdrivers; some of them have longer handles or a more comfortable grip, but every tool you're handed is still a screwdriver. Then someone hands you an electric drill. You still have to put the piece of furniture together, but man, how much easier it is with that electric drill!

The Daily Spend Limit is a methodology that engages us in a process that improves our habits and positions us for a better financial situation. It's a simple tool to help you navigate your everyday life with a budget that makes sense—one that you can actually stick to.

The Daily Spend Limit methodology presents an age-old concept in a way that better relates to our natural psychological desires. And I know that it works because it worked for me. When my wife and I implemented a Daily Spend Limit, we saw our savings grow. We saw our credit card bills drop to the lowest they'd been in a year. We became conscious of exactly how our choices were affecting our financial lives, and that awareness made a huge difference, both in our plans for the future and in our lives at the moment.

The Daily Spend Limit helps you own your finances by holding you accountable to your future, while also encouraging you to live your life today.

So what exactly is the Daily Spend Limit? It's a simple metric to abide by: one number that evolves as you do. The generally recommended practice of spending less and saving more is very hard to adhere to, but if you have a specific number to stick to, it becomes much easier. Humans don't tend to do well with generalizations. We are much better with specificity—and the Daily Spend Limit gives you that specificity.

In the simplest terms, the Daily Spend Limit is a specific dollar figure, a daily guilt-free spending amount. It's the amount you can spend every day on literally whatever you want. You don't have to worry about whether it's coming from your entertainment budget or coffee budget or travel budget. It is your everyday spending money, the amount you can spend every single day, no matter what.

How is this magical number calculated?

We analyze what you are making on a monthly basis and what you need to spend on a monthly basis in order to keep yourself alive; we include your weekly trips to the grocery store and even the gas station. Then we look at what you need for a solid financial future, free from debt and able to retire. Finally, we look at the wants you have for your future—buying a house, a new car, vacations—whatever you want.

Then we go to work. We analyze each piece of the equation to determine just how much of an allowance you can have to live life today, plan for the distant future, *and* build your life book full of experiences in the near future. We come up with one simple number that, if stuck to, allows you to own your financial situation instead of renting it: your Daily Spend Limit.

Your Daily Spend Limit is the exact dollar amount you can spend every day while covering your core expenses and achieving all your goals. That's right; spending a specific amount of money every day can actually help you achieve your goals!

Here's an example: Say you are thirty years old and live in Atlanta, and you have $15,000 in debt at a 19 percent interest rate. You make $50,000 a year, have $1,500 in core expenses each month, and would like to spend $1,200 on vacations each year. You also want to make sure you have $100,000 saved by the time you are forty-five. With a Daily Spend Limit of $24 a day, based on typical living expenses in Atlanta, you can actually achieve all of these goals. You can travel annually, meet your monthly expenses, be on track to meet that $100,000 goal, *and* pay off your debt in five years. All you have to do is stick to that one simple number.

We use our algorithm to figure out how to reach all of your goals in the most timely and efficient manner possible. Of course, you can't accomplish a thousand goals in six months; you have to be practical and space out your goals so that they are actually achievable. If you have $15,000 in debt and you make $50,000 a year, and you're looking to pay down your debt in two years, *and* you want to go on vacation in eight months, *and* you want to retire by the age of forty-five, your Daily Spend Limit is not going to be $500 a day.

The Daily Spend Limit is not a magic bullet. You still have to make a concerted effort to stick to it. If you continually go over your limit, your goals are going to be pushed back. But the Daily Spend Limit can guide you and help you figure out how to accomplish those goals so that you do get to them all eventually. It can help you reach your goals in the shortest time possible while still living your life today.

So how does the Daily Spend Limit work in practice? It's very simple. Your Daily Spend Limit is what you can spend each day, and you can spend it on whatever you want. Spend it all today on a new electronic device or spend a portion of it every day at Starbucks; the Daily Spend Limit doesn't care. You don't need to categorize every single transaction. You don't need to set your coffee limit for August or your dining-out spending for October. Simply plan your weeks or days around what you want to do that day or in the coming days. If you want to have a blowout weekend, then hold off on spending money Monday through Thursday and go out on the town on Friday. Or maybe you just need your Starbucks every morning; that's totally fine. Just stay within your Daily Spend Limit.

Say your Daily Spend Limit is $24 a day. That's the only number you have to remember. That's your high-water mark. In the morning, you swing by Starbucks and spend $4 on a coffee and $3 on a croissant. That's $7. Then you spend $15 on lunch. Now you're at $22. You know you're eating at home tonight and you're still a couple bucks below your Daily Spend Limit, so you treat yourself to a magazine on the way home and go to sleep that night comfortable in the knowledge that you've stayed within your limit.

You may be thinking, "It's impossible to stick to one exact number every single day." We agree; every day is different, and you spend a different amount every day. But if you are under on some days, then on other days, you can go over the limit. As long as it all averages out, you will be fine. Perhaps one day you bring your lunch from home, and instead of going out to eat, you spend that $15 on a cool T-shirt you've been eyeing; by bagging your lunch, you've stayed within your limit for that day.

Or perhaps you don't spend that $15 on anything. That means you'll have that $15 added to your Daily Spend Limit tomorrow, or whenever you want to use it. If your Daily Spend Limit is $24 and you only spend $10 a day during the week, all of sudden you have a hundred bucks to blow on the weekend!

The wonderful thing is that it also works in reverse. Say that you've spent $15 of your $24 Daily Spend Limit. Then a friend you haven't seen in a while texts you and asks if you want to get a drink after work. So you go, have a couple drinks, and *bam*—you are $10 over your Daily Spend Limit. Don't worry. The beauty of the Daily Spend Limit is that this is easy to remedy. All you have to do is adjust your spending for the next couple of days. If you were planning on buying lunch out tomorrow, bring it from home instead, and there you go: you're back on track. Even if you go over by more than just $10, you can still get back on track by adjusting your Daily Spend Limit for the next few days.

Of course, you can't splurge *all* the time, but the Daily Spend Limit makes it OK to splurge every once in a while. It makes it all right to live life day to day, without having to worry about every little thing all the time. You don't have to be the strictest person with the greatest self-control in the world in order to stick to the Daily Spend Limit. It's not meant to be stringent; it's just meant to be a simple baseline.

The Daily Spend Limit is extremely flexible because your life is fluid. You probably don't know what all your goals are right now, and you can't predict every trip you're going to want to take in the next five years—but that's OK. You can add in experiences you want to save for as you go. Every trip you decide you want to save up for becomes another goal with a set amount you want to save. We build in how much you need to save per month to accomplish that goal.

Your Daily Spend Limit is set so you know what your limit is for the entire month ahead. If you add a new goal mid-month, that will be factored into the next month's Daily Spend Limit. That way, you can plan for the month ahead, knowing what next week's Daily Spend Limit will look like. And each month, you'll have a fresh start that will allow you to meet your goals for that period.

Of course, your plans and goals may change—and that's just fine! Maybe you have been planning a trip to Paris, but then your friends invite you to their destination wedding in Hawaii, so you decide to push the Paris trip into the future by a couple years and go on the Hawaii trip instead. No problem—you can adjust and reschedule and add in new goals anytime you want. If you're browsing the Ticketmaster website and come across a concert that you didn't know about, but really want to go to, you can go ahead and add that to your goals, and your Daily Spend Limit will adjust so that you can pay for the ticket.

The Daily Spend Limit also helps you build up your cash reserves so that you can make those impulse purchases. If you see that concert ticket and want to buy it right now, go ahead and do it. Then simply adjust your Daily Spend Limit so that you'll pay yourself back for that purchase over the next month. By the time the day of the concert arrives, you'll have paid yourself back completely, and you can enjoy the experience knowing that it didn't hurt your finances at all.

The Daily Spend Limit helps you pay for those future experiences, even if you are actually spending the money today. In our survey, we found that most people start planning their vacations about six months in advance. Your trip may be six months away, but you start having to pay for things as soon as you start planning—booking flights, hotels, rental cars, and whatever else. How are you supposed to set a goal for something that you have to pay for in advance?

The first thing you should do is plan how much you would like to spend in total. Then you can spend that amount of money today, as you plan your trip, using the cash from your cash reserve, and you can set the actual date of the trip as your goal for when you are going to pay yourself back all that money. Your Daily Spend Limit will adjust so that by the time you get on that plane, you will have paid the whole trip off.

Life changes and evolves, and your budget should, too. Sometimes you may find that a goal you've been saving for isn't something you want anymore, and you want to save for something different. The Daily Spend Limit can adjust for that. Nothing is set in stone. Maybe you thought you wanted to retire at fifty-five, but you decide you actually would like to work until you're sixty. You can go ahead and change that and see how it affects your plan.

If your income situation changes—if you lose your job or you get a raise—your Daily Spend Limit will adjust accordingly. And if your core expenses change—if your rent goes up, or you cut cable and your Comcast bill goes down—your Daily Spend Limit is adjusted for that as well. Of course, your Daily Spend Limit will go up if you get a raise—but you could also elect to keep it the same and put that extra money toward meeting your goals sooner.

And what happens when that biggest budget obstacle comes up: when life gets in the way? Will everything come to a screeching halt? With the Daily Spend Limit, the answer is *no.* If you have to buy a last-minute plane ticket for $700 to deal with a family emergency, your Daily Spend Limit shouldn't drop to zero. You just need to pay yourself back, and you can do that by simply adding paying yourself back to the goals you already have, which will reduce your Daily Spend Limit accordingly. This allows you to continue living your life instead of saying, "We can't spend any money at all because we already spent it on this life event." You can still spend money; the amount is just slightly reduced until you've paid yourself back.

A traditional budget mind-set would tell you that you have to pay yourself back as quickly as possible, so for the next two months, you can't spend anything. But what if, instead of trying to pay yourself back *immediately*, you set a goal of four months, or six months? You'll still pay yourself back, but you'll be able to continue living your life in the meantime. You can integrate life into your life instead of letting life interrupt your life.

Your life is always evolving, and therefore your budget needs to be constantly evolving as well. Life happens, and your budget needs to be able to adjust to whatever happens. Owning your finances means that as life events arise, you can build them into your already-defined plan. Even if you get off track a couple months in a row, you can still jump back on again. You just have to adjust your Daily Spend Limit and stick to that new limit. Perhaps you have a big, ongoing life event, like a wedding or building a house, that will regularly require large, unusual cash expenditures for a period of time. Well, things are just going to be out of whack for a few months, and that's OK! Once things settle down, you can reexamine your goals, adjust your plans, set a new Daily Spend Limit, and get yourself back on track.

You may be thinking, *This is way too easy to work.* But that's the whole point! All it takes is very simple math and a little self-control. Many people think things have to be complex in order to work, but I don't believe that at all. A system doesn't have to be hard in order to be valuable. Finances become complicated when there are layers upon layers upon layers. People try to fix their behavior by making things more complicated, but really, it's simplicity that helps you create new habits. You have enough complexity in your life; managing your budget should be simple.

As we said in the last chapter, in order for something to become a habit, it has to be easy, normal, and rewarding. The Daily Spend Limit checks all three of these boxes, providing you with a solution that no other budgeting tool offers. No more burdensome complexity in your budget. Just one easy-to-remember number that you can easily check to determine whether to make a purchase or not. No need to navigate your complex, multi-line budget every time you need to make a spending decision. You don't have to remember your expense limits for fifteen different categories; your brain can't hold that many things in balance all the time anyway. You just have to remember one number.

If you want to take even greater ownership of your Daily Spend Limit, you can categorize your spending to better understand where you are trending higher and where you are doing really well, but it's not necessary to do that every single week, or even every month, in order to stick to a budget. The Daily Spend Limit provides you with a metric, not another avenue that needs maintenance. It's not something that you have to work on every single day. It makes it easier to live your life, to keep moving, knowing that your budget will move along with you, without having to spend an hour on it every weekend. It's a budget that works on the go.

Once you have it all set up, it's easy. You add new goals, make adjustments, check what your new Daily Spend Limit is, and move forward. You don't have to engage with the whole setup on a daily, weekly, or even monthly basis. You can just deal with that one number. As long as the groundwork has been done—identifying income sources, core expenses, and saving goals—then ongoing maintenance of the Daily Spend Limit is simply a matter of sticking to the plan and making adjustments when necessary.

Mark Zuckerberg famously said that he wore the same gray T-shirt every day so that he never had to think about his wardrobe, which freed him to use that brainpower on more productive things. That's what the Daily Spend Limit does. You know you're able to spend the same amount every day, so you can take the time and energy you would have spent on budgeting and spend it on other things.

It's easy to integrate the Daily Spend Limit into your normal life because people actually do these calculations naturally, even without a Daily Spend Limit. If you have a blowout weekend and spend a lot of money, you are probably going to take it easy for the next few days. You will naturally think, *Wow, I spent a lot of money this weekend, so I'm going to bring my lunch to work with me the next few days and cook dinner at home instead of eating out.* We have a natural cognizance of the money we spend. The Daily Spend Limit just integrates that with a holistic picture of your whole financial plan. Instead of trying to think about your entire life and your comprehensive financial plan every single day, you can just do one simple thing. Because the Daily Spend Limit is just one number, you can make it part of your daily life without spending a ton of time thinking about it. That's why it's a *Daily* Spend Limit instead of a Weekly or Monthly Spend Limit. It's much easier to remember what we spend in one day than what we spend in a week, never mind a month. You can keep a daily number in your head pretty easily.

Moreover, having this daily goal provides a daily reward. At the end of every day, you have the instant gratification of knowing that you succeeded in sticking to your Daily Spend Limit. And if you didn't, you have motivation to do better tomorrow because you instantly understand what you need to do to get back on track.

Every day, you get to start fresh. And at the end of every day, you get to assess how you did. Did I stay within my limit? Did I progress toward my goals? Do I need to make any changes tomorrow? And you can go to sleep knowing that everything will fall into place because you've factored in your savings, your future plans, and your core expenses. It's all covered.

Our minds will more willingly engage with something if it's rewarding. Not spending money is not rewarding—at least not immediately—but spending money *definitely* is! So we are naturally going to better stick to a budget that allows us to spend money. Conventional budgeting feels restrictive, which conflicts with our internal desires. With the Daily Spend Limit, we have created a single number that tells you what you *can* spend, rather than what you *can't* spend. By building in your needed savings and accounting for your core expenses, the Daily Spend Limit is a budget that says "yes," instead of consistently saying "no." You don't have to try to work out how going out for drinks is going to affect your ability to pay your rent. All of that complicated math is already taken care of. The only math you have to do is remembering whether or not you've spent less than that one easy-to-remember number.

If you stick to your Daily Spend Limit every day, it will start to become a habit. You don't have to actively think about sticking to your $50 or $25 a day; it becomes automatic. In Kahneman and Tversky's model, it becomes System 1 instead of System 2—automatic, instinctual, and habitual.

At the same time, the more you use it, the more you become aware of your spending habits, which helps you make better spending decisions. It gives you an understanding of how every spending decision affects your financial goals and dreams down the road. And this understanding enables you to easily make the best decisions.

Life would be easier in some ways if human beings acted almost like robots—if we weighed all costs against all benefits in order to reach the best decisions. But human beings are not robots. We generally don't make decisions based on rational, detached analysis, but rather on instinctive, emotional responses to our environment. Then, afterward, we rationalize those decisions to ourselves and to the outside world.

In order to change your behavior and make better decisions, you need cues to motivate you to act differently. When you are driving and see a light turn yellow as you approach an intersection, you are cued to make a decision: either slow down in anticipation of the coming red light or speed up to make it through the intersection before the light changes. Yellow makes you think about that decision.

You need similar cues when it comes to spending money. Budgets as they work now don't provide them. The math is far too complicated. There are so many different factors to consider, so many different categories to remember, that we don't have that reliable, identifiable cue. Instead, we think, *I'm not going to change my behavior because I won't really know the outcome of this spending decision until the end of the month.*

The Daily Spend Limit acts like that yellow light. It's simple to understand, so when you are about to make a purchase, you have an easy cue that prompts you to think, *Will I go over my Daily Spend Limit if I make this purchase?* It's a simple question. It's not about maintaining a budget on a daily basis; it's about providing you with a cue that you can remember easily every day—a cue that allows you to better understand how today's spending decisions will affect future spending decisions.

The Daily Spend Limit is a rolling benchmark that spurs you to think about how your daily transactions affect your short-, mid-, and long-term plans and goals. It's a cue that triggers you to think twice when you pull out your credit card. It prompts you to think, *Hmm, I want to go out this Saturday; maybe today I'll skip the Starbucks and drink the free coffee in the office so I can reserve some Daily Spend Limit dollars for the weekend.*

It's not about putting more processes into your everyday life. It's about adding *one* process, one cue that will trigger you to consider your spending activities. And that cue can help you create longer-term habits for yourself going forward.

"Now Matt," you may be saying to yourself at this point, "this all sounds great. The Daily Spend Limit seems like a wonderful tool. But how do I aggregate all that information to calculate my Daily Spend Limit number? And how am I actually supposed to implement it in my life?"

The answer is easy. His name is Benjamin.

Chapter Five

Meet Benjamin: The New Center of Your Financial Life

So, who is Benjamin?

Benjamin is an awesome dude. He's your true financial trainer. He's your accountability partner. He makes sure you get the valuable financial information and insight you need. He makes you feel comfortable dealing with your financial situation. He does it all with a smile—and he does it right from your computer or phone because, that's right: Benjamin is an app.

There are hundreds of budgeting and financial-planning apps out there. Why, you may ask, do we need one more?

The answer is, we don't. We don't need *one more* financial app; we need one financial app that *does more*—a holistic financial center that helps you integrate all aspects of your financial life. Instead of having a budgeting app, a round-up app, an investment app, a banking app—all these cooks in the kitchen telling you what to do—you just have one master chef, a commander in chief of your financial situation. Benjamin is that commander in chief.

It's not the ability to aggregate information that makes Benjamin unique. Plenty of platforms do that. Many of the personal financial-management apps out there claim to be one-stop shops. But usually, no matter how good the app is, it's missing one element or another.

For example, Mint also links to all your various financial accounts. It also allows you to set goals. But Mint doesn't connect all the pieces and analyze how they collectively affect the future of your financial situation. How does your investment portfolio interact with your goals? How does your credit card debt affect your retirement? How does saving for experiences interact with everything else?

Benjamin is different because he gives you insights on how all that information interacts. He doesn't just give you all the information; he shows you the holistic picture that information paints. He helps you better understand your financial life so that you don't have to take all these disparate pieces of information and figure out on your own what they mean.

Other apps do a good job of collecting information, but then they ask you to interpret it and decide what needs to be done next. They take all of these pieces of information, put them in front of you, and ask you to make a plan out of all of it. These apps can recommend goals, or they can tell you how much you need to save for retirement, but there are very few that can tell you how to make all the pieces work together in one comprehensive plan. That's fine if you're a financial analyst who can do all the math and understand how everything works. But for most of us, these apps don't give us the help we really need to make plans. Benjamin actually helps you make that plan. He helps you formulate a strategy that encompasses your core expenses, your future financial plans, and your savings goals, while still letting you live life today. Benjamin integrates all your disjointed financial information into one comprehensive—and comprehensible—plan with clearly defined action steps.

Benjamin can integrate the core aspects of your financial life into a holistic whole—saving, spending, investing, goal planning, and living your life today. He is the guide helping you to accomplish your goals and desired experiences while also shepherding you toward retirement and helping you cultivate better spending and saving habits. He helps you gain insight into your current situation while nudging you to become better in the future. Instead of using four different apps to figure out how one decision affects all the various aspects of your financial life, you can use just one app to obtain all that information.

The purpose of Benjamin is to be the center of your financial universe. He can be the best source of truth when it comes to your financial situation because we built him to have all the knowledge he needs.

To create Benjamin, we, the Wela team, drew on all the knowledge and experience we've accumulated in the course of our careers as financial advisors. We started by looking at our conversations with clients from the first meeting onward. When a prospective client sits across the table from an advisor, the advisor pulls from a deep well of both knowledge and intuition. We dug deep into the natural intuition that advisors develop by doing this job for decades, and we broke down every element of that conversation into the smallest pieces of information we could. Breaking things down allowed us to train Benjamin to handle different situations in order to devise an appropriate plan for every client individually.

Financial planning is holistic. It takes into account many different things: insurance, tax planning, investment planning, estate planning, retirement planning, and more. We broke down the whole relationship and asked ourselves a series of questions in order to get the clearest possible picture of what we needed Benjamin to do.

The first question we asked was, "Where does the conversation need to start in order for people to get to a place where all these other things are actually relevant?" The short answer to that question is "Savings." Now, usually when people come to us, they already have investible assets saved, so we move straight to the next stage—but we wanted to be sure that we started from the beginning so that we could encompass all people, whether or not they had investible assets saved already. That conversation starts with spending and saving, so that's where we wanted Benjamin to start. We determined what the core things are that people need to save for and spend on, and then built the necessary elements into Benjamin to help them do that.

There are four core foundational goals that you need to establish in order to build your financial plan:

1. Being cash flow positive—(You have to make more than you spend.)
2. Getting in line with credit card debt
3. Creating an emergency reserve
4. Saving for retirement

Those are the four core things that we need to help people achieve before we talk about anything else.

Having determined where the conversation needs to start, we asked ourselves another question: "What information do we need to position an individual to achieve those four goals?" For example, if we were sitting across the table from someone who had credit card debt, what would that conversation look like? (For the purpose of this example, we'll say that person is you.) First, we'd ask you how many credit cards you have, what the balance is on each of them, what the interest rate is on each of them, how much you are paying toward each credit card right now, and whether or not you still use the cards. Then we would analyze your answers to figure out how long it would take to pay off the credit card debt. We would look at your income. We would look at what you are paying in mortgage or rent; in utilities; for groceries; and for X, Y, and Z. We would also ask when you want to pay the credit card off. (Usually the answer is, "I want to pay it off yesterday!")

Then we would continue to break down that situation to find a solution. We would take either the credit card with the highest interest rate or the card that has the lowest balance—whichever worked better given all the other financial factors we're dealing with—and calculate when you could pay that card off with your free cash flow. That would be Stage One. Then, in Stage Two, we'd roll your cash flow over to your second credit card and get that one paid off. Then we'd move on to credit card number three.

We knew Benjamin needed to be able to do this—not just for credit card debt, but for the other four foundational goals as well. To determine exactly how to do that, he would need to analyze all the elements of your financial situation. Moreover, he would need to determine how this particular goal fit in with all of your other goals and financial plans.

In the world of person-to-person financial services, a financial advisor is the quarterback who leads you through everything. So we asked ourselves, how do we build that into an application? In order for a quarterback to be effective, he needs all the information in order to make a strategy work. The app would have to work the same way.

Information is at the core of how Benjamin works. When you set up Benjamin, you link all of your different financial accounts and providers to the app: your checking accounts, your savings accounts, your loan companies, your credit card companies, your investment accounts, your retirement accounts, your home value—every single element of your financial life. Benjamin is able to connect to accounts from 13,000 institutions, so he can aggregate information from just about everything. Benjamin then aggregates all this information and automatically generates a financial plan based on those four core foundational goals. He then determines how much you need to save for each of these goals in order to meet them within a particular period of time.

You may be thinking, "Can an app really create my financial plan—the plan that is supposed to help me fulfill my hopes and dreams?" The great thing about Benjamin is that he actually works *with* you. The plan Benjamin creates is built on aggregated information and assumptions that Benjamin makes based on that information. From there, you can make adjustments so that it reflects your personal plan even more accurately. You can adjust your desired retirement age. You can adjust when you'd like to pay off your credit card debt. If Benjamin is assuming a different interest rate on your credit card, or a different growth rate for your investments, or a different income level or mortgage payment, you can adjust all of those. Then, you put in the experiences you want to save for. You can add in your desired experiential goals—the trips you want to take, the things you want to do. He already has an understanding of what it would cost for you to get there, and he works those goals into your plan.

You take the base plan that Benjamin designs and fine-tune it to perfectly fit your financial life and goals. You work with Benjamin to create that financial plan, the big picture of where you want your financial life to be and where you want it to go. Benjamin then calculates the Daily Spend Limit that will allow you to achieve this plan.

The more information you give to Benjamin, the better he will be able to help you. And the best way to provide Benjamin with the information he needs is through linking your accounts. The longer you use him, the more he'll learn. But in the beginning, you may have to help him out and tell him where certain expenses or transactions fit in.

You don't have to link all of your accounts to Benjamin if you don't want to. You can enter transactions and information manually, and Benjamin will analyze the information you enter. But it won't be as consistent and ever evolving as it can be if you link everything to the platform. If you link all of your accounts, Benjamin is able to analyze everything for you and integrate it into your plan.

The more information you put into Benjamin, the more effective and helpful he will be. Benjamin creates a foundation for you just through the accounts you have linked. The more information you link, the better Benjamin understands your situation, and the deeper and more comprehensive your plans and goals will be.

The great thing is that as you work with Benjamin to develop your financial plan, he is busy doing all the complicated stuff: sorting through all the information and figuring out how it affects and contributes to achieving your financial goals. All the processes in the app are like worker bees. The worker bees analyze each of the bits and pieces of information, all the time, every day. One worker bee is constantly analyzing your income: is it the same this month as it was last month? One worker bee is constantly analyzing your mortgage payments: has the mortgage been paid yet this month? No? Then we can expect that to come out soon. One worker bee is analyzing credit card debt: did it move down as we assumed? You've got a worker bee for average credits for accounts, average debits for accounts, total expenses each month, rent expenses, credit card interest charges for the past three months, how much you need to retire, and so on.

The worker bees ask questions and gather answers. The credit-card-debt-goal worker bees ask: does the user have interest charges in the past 90 days? What percent of the user's income is the credit card balance? What is the Wela-approved level of debt for the user? What is the dollar amount to save toward credit card debt? How much are current credit card payments?

Then the controller, Benjamin, helps make decisions: is this person in trouble with credit card debt? How much debt does he or she need to pay off? How much can the user put toward credit card debt while still meeting daily living expenses? Based on the amount being paid toward credit card debt, when will he or she have it paid off? How is the user progressing toward getting the debt paid off?

The worker bees are constantly breaking down your financial situation based on the information input or aggregated and delivering the results to the controller—Benjamin. Benjamin can digest the information and learn from it. He sorts through all this information and figures out what needs to go to you, the user; what needs to go to your advisor; what needs to go back to another worker bee; and what can be disregarded for the time being. A lot of information is stashed away because you don't need *all* of the information every second of the day. Benjamin figures out what information you, the user, need right now to help you make the best progress.

Many financial-planning operations actually provide *too* much information—so much that you get completely overwhelmed. You can't possibly sort through that much information and make sense of it all, never mind figure out how to use it to put together a financial plan. With Benjamin, however, you can find the middle ground that gives you as much information as you want without totally inundating you until you're paralyzed and discouraged from taking action. Benjamin is as simple as you want him to be, but he is also transparent enough that you can go as deep as you want. You can dig into the details or you can stick to the information Benjamin presents to you—the information that he has determined will be most helpful based on your individual situation.

You'll get notifications on transactions that come in. Benjamin will automatically categorize them as core expenses or as daily expenses, but you can recategorize them if you see that Benjamin has made a mistake. If Benjamin is not sure how an expense should be categorized, he will ask where it should go—and then he will help you determine whether certain expenses are life expenses that should be built into the plan or whether they should be taken out of your Daily Spend Limit.

Benjamin lives, breathes, and evolves with you. Your life doesn't stand still, and neither does Benjamin. When you want to update something—to add an experience or to change goals—you can easily adjust things in Benjamin, and he can do all the math to help you achieve those goals. Benjamin adjusts your Daily Spend Limit for the next month, so you know what you need to do in the coming month. Every time you change something, all the little worker bees reanalyze every element and pass the results on to Benjamin, and Benjamin passes the plan on to you in the form of a revised Daily Spend Limit.

And you can adjust those variables as you go, whether it's, "I want to retire sooner than Benjamin has predicted," or, "I want to reach this experiential goal sooner than I originally desired," or whatever else. Benjamin is always evolving. The plan that you set with Benjamin today isn't going to be the same plan in fifteen years, or in five years, or next year, or even next month. It's going to change. Maybe you get a raise. Maybe you get married. Maybe you have kids. Perhaps you start out thinking that you will retire at seventy-five, but as your career progresses, you are able to save more toward your retirement and move your retirement age down to sixty-five.

You know that your plan will change, but that doesn't mean you shouldn't make one today. The plan you make today is your starting point, and Benjamin will help you continue to revise your plan as circumstances in your life evolve. In a way, it's like the app Waze. You put in your destination, and it gives you a route to take. You might end up deviating, and your estimated time of arrival might change during the course of your journey, but it gives you a map to follow, and you have a starting point to anchor you.

Because Benjamin can make those changes and help your plan evolve, you don't have to go to a financial advisor every time something in your life changes. Technology allows Benjamin to adapt your plan quickly and easily. Benjamin can automatically detect any changes in your regular monthly financial activity—for example, if your rent has gone up, or your car insurance has gone down, or you get a raise. If Benjamin sees a big change in your regular transactions, he'll check in to see if everything is all right or whether adjustments need to be made. Then he can adjust your Daily Spend Limit accordingly for the next month. You don't have to go back to your kitchen table, pull out your Excel spreadsheet, plug in all the new numbers, and do the math all over again. Benjamin does all that for you, automatically. He'll digest the new information and make adjustments starting the next month.

Benjamin is always there, and he's always working for you. Benjamin is like a financial advisor who only has one client: you. His entire day is built around ensuring that you are informed, held accountable, and progressing toward the plan you have set out to accomplish. He helps you steer when things get a little swervy. He helps you see when things get a little foggy.

We had a young couple as clients who were put into a great situation and given some good fortune at the company where they worked. The couple had a pair of young children who were heavily involved in sports. Every time the couple came to the office, we would talk about their spending and the withdrawals they were taking from their investment account.

This couple was given a great base, but they were starting to eat into it. Fortunately, the markets were high, so the impact wasn't too great at the time, but we wanted to prevent things from getting bad in the future. So we analyzed their budget and set a new budget that would keep them from withdrawing from their investment account.

A year later, they were back in our office, and we were having the exact same conversation. They weren't sticking to the budget we had come up with. Whether it was as result of the cost of sports equipment, or because their kids were eating through the pantry and they were spending more on food, or because they were eating out all the time as they traveled for their kids' sports events, they were building up credit card debt and blowing through their budget.

This went on and on. Every year, there was something else that would cause them to go off budget and dig into their investment account. And I started thinking, *Wouldn't it be great if I could be with these people every day? I've analyzed their budget and I know what their core expenses are; I could help them with their discretionary spending. We could talk and identify the things they bought that weren't needed, and I could help them figure out what to spend and how to spend so that they could achieve their goals.*

All of this happened before we had even developed the Daily Spend Limit—and it contained the seeds of the ideas behind Benjamin: someone who could be with you all the time, nudging you while you were in the moment. And with technology, we could actually do it.

Benjamin is always at your beck and call. If you're worried about something—if you wake up in the middle of the night thinking about something five years down the road, or if you're sitting on the beach on vacation and all of a sudden get worried about your retirement—you don't have to make an appointment or send an email and wait for a response. Instead, you can just ask Benjamin, and then you can take immediate action. Even if the answers are not quite what you wanted to hear, at least you have clarity. If you still want to make an appointment with an advisor, of course you can—but you can have answers and clarity right away.

Benjamin is always there to help answer those spur-of-the-moment financial questions. You can receive answers anytime and anywhere. Say it's halftime at your kids' soccer game, and you realize that you'd love to be able to spend more time with your kids sooner. Could you possibly retire at fifty-six instead of sixty-two? You can pull out Benjamin and immediately see what that would look like. Then, when you next meet with your financial advisor, guess what? Your financial advisor already knows what you've been thinking because he or she is tied into your Benjamin. Then the two of you can discuss your plan to make that happen.

Benjamin is not meant to replace humans when it comes to wealth management or financial services. A human financial advisor builds a relationship with you and mentors you psychologically; sometimes you need to know that there is a real human being you can talk to. Benjamin is just meant to make humans better at financial calculations—and he can actually help human financial advisors help their clients.

As a financial advisor, I can tell you: forty-five minutes of every meeting is data gathering. It's catching up on all the details of the client's financial situation. "Did you save for your kids' college fund last year? We talked about increasing your 401(k) to $15,000; did you do that? What's your mortgage balance? What's your current credit card debt?"

Now, imagine how differently that time could be spent if I had access to that client's Benjamin. I would already know all that information, so we wouldn't have to spend forty-five minutes rehashing all the details of my client's recent financial activities. Instead of focusing on the past, we could focus on what to do next, and on building a personal relationship.

The relationship is what people really value in a financial advisor: someone who knows them, who relates to them as a human being, and who honestly cares about helping them improve their financial situation. Benjamin enables financial advisors to be more efficient, and clients know their advisor won't forget any of their individual financial details because it's all there in Benjamin.

For example, an advisor can look at the information from Benjamin and see that their client is having a tough time paying down debt. The client has a plan but is having trouble sticking to it. The advisor can then decide how to proceed—whether the client needs a new plan, or whether it's a matter of working through a psychological barrier so the client can stick to the plan as it is.

Benjamin knows his limits and can tell you when you should talk to a financial advisor—and even set up a meeting with the appropriate advisor. Benjamin is focused on spending and saving, and on how that interacts with your entire financial situation. But if you are looking for specific investment advice, for instance, Benjamin will probably recommend that you talk to a financial advisor. He has the ability to ping you to say, "You're doing really well, and I think you could probably benefit even more by meeting with a financial planner for some investment advice." Or perhaps your fees look a little high, or your allocation seems a little off. Benjamin will see that and recommend that you talk to your financial advisor.

If your financial advisor has access to your Benjamin, he or she can also see if you need a face-to-face meeting. If we, at Wela, have an investment-management client, for example, Benjamin can tell us if that person didn't react well when Google dropped 5 percent. So when we see that Google is on the verge of dropping, we can contact our client to help him or her decide what to do.

However, many of the questions you might want to ask a financial advisor can be answered through simple analysis. So, instead of a time-consuming and intimidating meeting with a financial advisor, you can simply ask Benjamin and get your answer right away. And, when you do need to meet next with your financial advisor, you can rest assured that he or she has the same information as Benjamin.

One of the reasons people avoid meeting with financial advisors in the first place is that they don't feel like they know enough about their financial situation to make the time spent on a meeting worthwhile. Benjamin allays that insecurity. With Benjamin, you have all the information you need. No matter what is happening in your financial life, you can ease into a conversation with your advisor because you know that both you and your advisor have the same information.

You may feel intimidated by the prospect of dealing with your financial situation, but with Benjamin, there's no need to worry. All you have to do is link everything to Benjamin and let him sort it out for you. And you don't have to be intimidated by Benjamin, either. After all, he's just an app! (And a very secure one at that!)

No matter what, Benjamin is always on your side. He's here to help you and hold your hand. Come hell or high water, Benjamin has got your back.

Chapter Six

How Can Benjamin Help Me?

Benjamin sounds pretty great, right? But how exactly does he help you, specifically? How does he make a difference in your day-to-day life?

Benjamin is designed to help you positively change financial behaviors in small, bite-size ways that allow you to have ownership in the process. He's built with an understanding of advanced behavioral economic theories, which enables him to nudge you toward situations and habits that will better you financially. Benjamin allows you to gradually progress toward your long-term financial goals and still have many smaller wins along the way.

Benjamin wants to keep you from going all the way to one end of the spectrum or the other. He wants to keep you from spending all your money today and risking your future—but he also wants to prevent you from living *only* for the future, and not having any joy or good experiences today. Benjamin wants to help you live in the sweet spot between these two ways of life. That's the sweet spot of owning your finances.

The goal of Benjamin is not to get you to do less; the goal is to enable you to do more—without having to put in an inordinate and burdensome amount of work. Finance isn't fun; there's no arguing with that. But Benjamin eliminates the maintenance associated with budgeting. Instead of the headache of analysis, you have an engaging and intriguing interaction with Benjamin.

Benjamin's algorithms make the maintenance simple. All you need to focus on is execution. You don't have to worry about crunching numbers; Benjamin's got it. But in order for Benjamin to be successful, he requires action. He can't actually keep you from swiping your credit card or spending that cash. He's as silver bullet as it gets, but he's not too good to be true. The money in your pocket is *your* money, and Benjamin can't prevent you from spending it. But he can put a bug in your ear and nudge you to use your money better.

Benjamin doesn't want to tell you what to do. He isn't trying to control you or be Big Brother. He just provides insight and makes suggestions. He just wants to help you move in the right direction to better your financial situation today, tomorrow, and all the way down the line.

Benjamin is meant to be your confidant and accountability partner. He helps you become more aware of your financial situation, creating a stronger connection between you and your finances than you've had before. The information Benjamin gives you may not be the information you want to hear, but it's going to be the insight into your situation that you need. Awareness is the first step toward securing your financial present and future. If you don't know what's going on, then the Daily Spend Limit and all of the suggestions Benjamin can make will do no good.

In your first few weeks and months with Benjamin, you will probably have many epiphanies about your spending habits, and you will attain a much greater awareness of your financial situation. Benjamin will tell you where you are spending money and where you are not spending money.

One perfect example of a small thing with a big impact that Benjamin can make you aware of is micro spending. You think, *I'll spend $2.50 here; it's not that much.* But then you spend another $2.50 there, and another $2.50, and each time it doesn't seem like much, but it all adds up. And, all of a sudden, you've spent much more money than you meant to. Benjamin is there to keep track of those little expenses and make you aware of them. He can help you understand where you are spending the most money, where you are spending the least money, where you've improved, and where you may have fallen behind. He is consistently analyzing, determining whether a given expense will cause you to stray from your longer-term vision, and figuring out ways to encourage you to do the right thing.

Benjamin helps you keep moving toward all of your goals, ensuring that you are sticking to your financial plan by utilizing the Daily Spend Limit. Benjamin is able to track and adjust your Daily Spend Limit and provide you with notifications and updates on it. What did you spend during the week? What can you spend over the weekend? Should you cut back the following week? How are you progressing toward your goals? Benjamin recalculates your Daily Spend Limit every single day based on what you've spent on the previous days. He tracks your transactions and automatically calculates how much of your Daily Spend Limit you have left. At the end of the day, he can tell you how much has rolled over to tomorrow—or how much you need to make up for if you went over your limit that day.

Of course, you don't have to log into your account every single day. You can see what your initial Daily Spend Limit is and just stick to that. And if you stay under or go over and want to check to see whether it's been readjusted, you can just log in to Benjamin and see where you are.

Benjamin can even predict your spending in advance. Because he knows your habits, he can guess at what your expenses will be in the coming week and help guide you. This is especially helpful because these in-between spans of time can often be the hardest to manage. You can grasp how much to spend today, or how much to spend this week, but it can be difficult to look ahead and predict how much you are going to spend in the next couple of weeks.

Benjamin can help with that. Using a machine-learning model based on multiple variables, Benjamin is able to predict what you will likely spend up to seven days in advance. He can say, "All right, we can see that you are going to spend $1,000 in the coming week. Given your Daily Spend Limit, that means you are going to be in a tough spending position at the end of the week. So, I'm going to set your limit for the week at $750, to position you better in the future."

Benjamin can help ensure that you make it through the week—and still get the weekend you want. Everybody looks forward to the weekend, right? And everybody worries about having money to spend on the weekend. Benjamin can tell you exactly how much you can spend and still have enough left over to enjoy the weekend.

Again, these calculations are something we do even without Benjamin, albeit very roughly. If we go out and make a big purchase, or have a big night out, we know we should hold off on spending money over the next few days. But we generally don't know *how much* or *for how long* we should hold off. We just hold off until we feel better—which is usually a couple of days—and then we go back to spending.

With Benjamin, you know how much to hold off. You can check Benjamin, and say, "OK, I have been really good about bringing my lunch to work this week. I can afford to eat lunch out today and still go to that nightclub this weekend."

Ultimately, Benjamin wants to help you normalize your spending over the course of the month. Normalization allows for consistency, but also flexibility. Most budgets are completely inflexible—you have to stick to your budget no matter what, or the whole thing is ruined and useless.

But not every day is the same. Not every week is the same. Maybe you have a week coming up when you know you are going to be spending a lot of money. Benjamin can help you figure out what to spend for the two weeks prior, so that you have the money to spare for that more expensive week.

In a traditional budget, you'd have to figure out where to cut from in order to plan for that extra spending. "All right, I can cut $10 from my entertainment budget, $10 from my food budget..." You have to do all sorts of math to figure out how to cover those two weeks. And if you don't quite estimate correctly, then afterward, you have to recalculate all over again. With Benjamin, all you have to pay attention to is your Daily Spend Limit, which is constantly evolving.

And if, after you've spent that money, your Daily Spend Limit is too low for you to get by, you can call it a life transaction and build in a goal of paying yourself back over a longer period of time. You can tell Benjamin, "These are life transactions. They will eat into my emergency reserve, and I will have to build it back up." Or you can tell Benjamin, "I will pay this back next month because I know I'm getting a big quarterly bonus check." When life happens, Benjamin can automatically add in a goal of paying yourself back. He'll calculate what it means for your Daily Spend Limit and implement that into your Daily Spend Limit for the next month. Then you don't even have to think about paying yourself back, or about the stress of covering for that life event. You just keep living your life with your adjusted Daily Spend Limit.

Benjamin can help you make those day-to-day, week-to-week, and month-to-month decisions. Should you hold off on saving for that goal in order to get your credit card balance back down to zero? Benjamin can help you decide. If you see that Best Buy is having a big sale and you want to buy that cool gadget you've wanted, you can go into Benjamin and see what it would look like to make that purchase today—how it would affect your Daily Spend Limit and what it would take to pay yourself back—and you can decide whether now is the time to buy, or not.

And if you make a poor choice, if you get off track, Benjamin makes it easy to get back on. He'll tell you what you need to do to get back on target with your plan and your longer-term goals—or what adjustments you need to make to your plan to make it achievable.

In some ways, the way Benjamin works is similar to a GPS: If you enter a destination into your phone or your standalone GPS at the beginning of your trip, but then you deviate from the prescribed route—maybe because there's a construction detour, or you simply make a wrong turn—the GPS doesn't just give you up for lost; it recalculates. (Older models actually used to say "recalculating" out loud in a nasal, judgmental voice.) It finds the best route to where you want to be from where you are now, regardless of how far off track you may have gotten.

If life happens, if you get off track, Benjamin can automatically recalculate and tell you how to move forward. And you don't have to feel any shame or guilt. Benjamin won't judge you for getting off track. You don't have to call up an advisor or look anybody in the eye and say, "I know I got off track. I'm ready to get back on now." It's between you and Benjamin. And Benjamin will never judge you.

Benjamin is meant to reduce anxiety so that you can seek the financial advice you need, no matter what your situation looks like. Too often, people shy away from financial advisors because they feel they have made foolish decisions and they fear being judged. Benjamin allays these fears.

You can ask Benjamin any question you want, any time you want. The interaction with Benjamin is via chat bot. You open the app, click on Benjamin's face, and he presents you with a whole assortment of questions you can select to ask that he can then answer. The conversation can be as long or as short as you want.

And if you don't know what questions to ask, don't worry. Benjamin actually comes with pre-populated questions to guide you, such as, "How am I doing on my Daily Spend Limit? When am I going to run out on my Daily Spend Limit for the month? What are my top expenses? What can I cut to keep true to my limits?" He presents you with the questions that you might not know to ask.

You can use Benjamin on your own time; he's always there. You can check Benjamin every day—but you also don't have to. As long as he has all the information he needs—as long as you have him all set up and linked to all your accounts—he'll just keep trucking along, whether you check him or not. Check him daily, check him weekly, or check him monthly; he'll be ready.

Benjamin is not going to hound you or annoy you unless there is something urgent that needs your attention. But if Benjamin doesn't proactively tell you that you need to do something, then you know you can just stay on track with your Daily Spend Limit.

You don't have to interact with Benjamin. But the more you use him, the better he will get and the more useful he will be. In any relationship, the longer you know a person, the less that has to be explained, and the more you understand. It's the same with Benjamin. The more information you provide Benjamin, and the more you use him, the more insightful and helpful he gets, and the more able he is to give you a seamless, cohesive financial experience.

Moreover, the more you interact, the more invested in the process you will become, and the more likely you will be to stick with it long-term. The more we put into something, the more committed we are to it. For example, in the 1930s, a well-known company came out with a revolutionary product: easy cake in a box. All you did was throw everything in the box into a pan, add water, and bake it. You didn't really have to do anything else. The company thought people would love it—but it completely flopped. So the company made an adjustment: they required that you mix in an egg before putting it into the oven. With that adjustment, the cakes started selling like, well, hotcakes.

Why did this happen? Because of something called the IKEA effect. We feel more of a connection to something and more ownership of it if we have some hand in actually building or creating it—if we have actually put some sort of equity into it. That's one reason people love their IKEA furniture so much. With the first cake in a box, people felt like they didn't have a hand in baking anymore. "I'm just throwing this in there; I'm not owning any of this process. I've basically been cut out." And this is why some people are averse to using apps that do everything for you; they want to still have some ownership to feel like they are doing something active to better themselves.

That's the challenge that all technology companies face at times: making things as simple as possible, while still allowing the user to have some ownership in the process. That's why Benjamin is so transparent. There's no, "Don't look at the man behind the curtain," with Benjamin. You can look behind the curtain and make sure that Benjamin is on track. The elements are exposed so that you can go in and look at them and have as much ownership and control as you'd like. We find that many users like to go in and enter the numbers, to see them and touch them and feel them. Then we feel more committed because we are more invested in the process.

We live in a world in which much of what we do is detached from physical reality. The further we get from physical things, the more ill-adapted we are to actually handling them. It's hard to attach tangible value to virtual money. Physical money feels more real. And people often have an easier time budgeting when they have something physical to which they can relate.

This is one of the reasons so many people still use a pencil and paper to budget. In our survey, we found that over 33 percent of individuals who have a budget maintain that budget via pencil and paper. And over 40 percent of individuals making less than $100,000 a year who have a budget maintain their budget via pencil and paper. Why is this? Because people feel they have more ownership when they are maintaining their budget via physical means as opposed to an electronic tool.

A study on saving was performed on the residents of a slum in Kenya. The subjects of the study were offered various types of incentives to save. One incentive was that if they saved a certain amount, they would get a bonus. Other subjects were given a bonus in advance, and money was taken away if they did not save. Some were sent emotional letters from family members and loved ones urging them to save. And some were given a little coin, and each time they saved, they'd make a scratch on the coin.

All of these incentives were effective to some degree, but the most effective was physically scratching the coin to record their savings.[2] The physical act of scratching the coin became a cue for the person to remember to save and did more to encourage saving than any of the other incentives.

2. "Case Studies: The Coin Study," Center for Advanced Hindsight, accessed March 7, 2018. www.advanced-hindsight.com/case-studies/the-coin-study/

Benjamin is intended to have that tangible effect—to provide that physical reinforcement that helps you stick to your budget. Benjamin helps with this engagement through notifications. We are all very busy, and we tend to fall into the "out of sight, out of mind" trap. Now, we don't need thirty push notifications every day to remind us; we just need that one simple cue, like the scratched coin. While the Daily Spend Limit is not physical, it is one simple task that you can fulfill—and every time you make a scratch, you feel a sense of accomplishment.

Benjamin allows you to gamify the process of spending and saving. We all know that feeling: every time we beat a level on one of those little games on our phone, we feel good and we want to play the next level. It's addicting. What if we could make saving feel the same way? If you follow the rules of the game—i.e., the Daily Spend Limit—you will win the game this week, and you'll derive enormous satisfaction from winning.

Benjamin allows you to reward yourself for winning the game—that is, for making smart decisions. Stay under your Daily Spend Limit during the week and reward yourself by splurging on the weekend. Stick to a reduced Daily Spend Limit for a few months and reward yourself with that trip to Rome.

Benjamin knows that rewarding experiences make for a fulfilling life. And that's what Benjamin wants for you: an exciting, fulfilling life, today and in the future.

Chapter Seven

Your Spouse Spends Too Much? Let Benjamin Straighten Him (or Her) Out

Finances are often a big source of tension in a relationship. The financial conversation with a spouse tends to be the most difficult conversation to have. It can get really sticky and awkward. You don't want to tell your spouse what to do, but you also know that you both need to be on the same page about your finances.

Finances are one of the most private things to an individual. Talking about money is taboo in our society. With our culture's focus on keeping up with the Joneses, nobody wants to show his cards. People want to continue to play the game of poker, either bluffing or never turning over their hand. Everybody is afraid of being judged—even by his or her own spouse. People don't want to be told what they can and can't do with their money, and they don't want to be judged, whether they're in a bad situation or a good situation.

People work hard for their money, so they don't want to be told that they're not doing a good job of tending it. They want ownership of their own finances, even when they're married. Controlling your own finances means freedom. Someone else, even your significant other—sometimes *especially* your significant other—telling you what to do with your money often feels incredibly restricting. It also feels judgmental and untrusting, as though your significant other doesn't trust you to manage your own money.

Nobody likes to be micromanaged in any aspect of his or her life. We hate to be micromanaged when it comes to where we spend our money, and it's only natural that we dislike other people telling us what to do. So even if we know that our spouse is the one who has all the numbers in his or her head, who is keeping track of the budget and everything, if he or she tells us what we can or can't spend, we still want to bark back, "Don't tell me what to do!"

It can feel demeaning to be told how to spend your money, and it can be frustrating to try to get your significant other to understand why you want him or her to spend or save in a certain way. When people feel either demeaned or frustrated, they naturally get defensive and fight back, and things can easily blow up into an argument.

People have very strong opinions on how to spend money and how to manage finances. They have different ideas about where to spend and where to save. It's like a relationship's version of opposing political opinions. People come down on one side of an issue or another, and it's nearly impossible to make them see the other side.

No matter who's earning the money, we all have our own views regarding how it should be properly managed, and we often feel that the other side's views are wrong. *My spouse doesn't manage money the right way,* we think, *because it's not my way, and my way is the only way to do it. I do X, Y, and Z with my money. My spouse does X, Y, and Z with his/her money, and feels he/she is doing it the right way.* Each tries to convince the other of his or her views, but views on money are deeply ingrained. We learn them early based on our family's situation, and our own situation slightly later in life. And so the conversation tends to spiral into an argument.

People don't want to have the hard conversation because they are afraid of getting into a fight. They're scared of what the other person is going to say, so they don't even want to broach the topic. They don't want to come close to it. They want to find the easiest solution because they just want to avoid having a difficult conversation. And the easiest solution is to just keep everything separate.

In fact, a 2014 survey found that more and more millennials have bank accounts separate from their spouses. There are many reasons for this, but one of the roots is a lack of desire to talk about individual finances. People want to avoid a very uncomfortable conversation, so they keep things separate and put off important planning for the future.[3]

It's really no different than the way individuals avoid putting together a financial plan and tackling financial goals: because we believe that we will be able to deal with them later. We figure that we have plenty of time. The same is true in a relationship. *Everything's fine right now,* we think. *I don't want to rock the boat.* We figure that if we just keep things to ourselves, it will all work out . . . until it doesn't.

This happens frequently in business as well. That's why, over the past two years, I've been specifically committed to being very communicative with our team. Prior to this, I felt that if I was talking to people one on one, or if we just executed actions individually, then there was no need to open up to the whole team about cross-functional aspects.

But that wasn't the case. There are many more advantages to communicating across the whole team, both when things are

3. "TD Bank Survey Finds Many Couples Maintain Separate Bank Accounts," March 24, 2014, www.prnewswire.com/news-releases/td-bank-survey-finds-many-couples-maintain-separate-bank-accounts-251917121.html.

difficult and when things are going well. Communication is key, and often we don't realize it until we need to communicate about something going wrong. We don't realize that communication when things are good, when there are no fires to put out, will help us communicate more easily when there *are* fires.

Most of us have had those moments at work when a fire starts, and there hasn't been any communication. *I wish I'd been told some of these things before!* we usually think. *Then I could have done something about this situation. Now it's too late, and I can't do anything.* If more communication had taken place earlier, before the fire, the fire probably could have been avoided—or at least we would be able to do something about it now.

The same thing happens with our personal finances. Ultimately, if you can't talk together as a couple about your longer-term financial situation, your financial goals—regardless of whether or not you have joint accounts—then things are eventually going to collapse. You will reach a breaking point when it comes to your finances, and if you're not able to have the conversation when things are good, you are definitely not going to have it when things are bad.

We've all fought with our significant other about money, whether it's spending too much here or not saving enough there. It's completely normal. Everybody does it. My wife and I have certainly had those arguments. "Why are you spending so much here? Why are you spending so much there?" And we each think, as the recipient of such questions, *Get off my back! It's my money; I earned it!*

When we started using the Daily Spend Limit, that fight went out the window. We didn't care where the other one was spending his or her money, because as long as we each stayed within our personal Daily Spend Limit, everything was fine!

Benjamin provides a common language to make those inevitable and necessary conversations more manageable and more valuable. He can be the mediator. Benjamin has no emotions. He doesn't take a side. So he can be the impartial referee, the be all and end all of an argument.

Opinions about money are often painted as one of the fundamental make-or-break elements of a relationship. If you have differing opinions on how to manage money, it is seen as an irreconcilable difference. And yet, as they say, opposites attract. It's a cliché, but it's often true: in a couple, compatibility often comes from one person being the yin and one the yang.

In terms of finances, I find that many couples end up with a nerd and a free bird. Nerds like to budget because they want to ensure that they are saving toward future goals and objectives. Free birds want to enjoy life today and feel like budgets restrict them too much. This is certainly true in my relationship: I'm definitely the nerd, while my wife is the free bird. She wants to spend money to enjoy life today, and I want to save to ensure our future.

So often, budgets only allow for one way of life, one way of managing money. It's set in stone and can't budge. There's no room for both the yin and the yang. But with Benjamin, we both get what we want. Benjamin allows the nerd to plan and set saving goals and feel comfortable that everything is going the way it should—that all the goals will be met and their future will be secure. But it also allows the free bird to spend money—within the Daily Spend Limit, of course, but that money can still be spent without guilt. With Benjamin, the nerd has a built-in budget for goals, and can add goals and adjust as needed. The free bird has a Daily Spend Limit to enjoy life today without impacting the nerd's plans for the future.

With a regular budget, if life happens, the nerd is going to say, "We need to cut out all the fun stuff." No more dinner with friends, no more sushi on Tuesday nights, nothing except recovering from that life event. You can imagine how much this would pain the free bird, and what arguments might ensue because of it.

Because Benjamin sorts out how to cover those life events while still being able to spend money, you can avoid that argument entirely. The nerd can rest assured that the expense is covered, and the free bird can keep his or her Tuesday sushi nights. Everybody wins.

The nerd doesn't have to worry about what the free bird is spending his or her money on, and the amount doesn't matter as long as it falls within the Daily Spend Limit. It could be spent on lunch every day, on new shoes, on going to the movies, on whatever the free bird would like. Because it is within the Daily Spend Limit, it has no effect on the financial plans and goals of the nerd. So the free bird doesn't have to worry about the nerd getting upset about the former's spending of money, no matter what it's spent on.

Everybody values things differently. There's no universal rule on what should have the most value. What I think is worth spending money on may seem totally not worth it to you. Perhaps I want to go out for dinner or drinks with my friends multiple nights a week. To you, that may be an irresponsible way to spend money. But to me, those friendships and that social time is incredibly valuable.

If you want to save money for a Jet Ski and your spouse doesn't want to, you can factor into Benjamin to save for the Jet Ski out of your own Daily Spend Limit. Then there can be no argument about spending $3,000 on a Jet Ski, because you were able to save for it without affecting either your spouse's spending or your future financial plans and goals.

With the Daily Spend Limit, we can both spend our discretionary money on whatever we value. My wife can go to

Target with her Daily Spend Limit and spend it all on whatever she likes. And then we can talk over dinner about what we spent our Daily Spend Limit on and not get stressed about what the other person might think about how we spent our money. We can both spend on what makes us happy, knowing that everything is in place to make our future successful. And if one of us does go over our limit, we can focus the conversation on the Daily Spend Limit, as opposed to making value judgments about what the other person is spending money on.

Often, one person in a relationship makes more money than the other. You are almost certainly not going to put the exact same amount toward your expenses, savings, and future goals. Benjamin can help figure out how to handle joint expenses, even if your finances are kept separate, whether it's buying a house or caring for children or saving for your kids' college. He can help provide a common ground for building your future together.

Even if you do want to keep your finances separate, if you are married, there are going to be those same joint aspects of your financial situation, and financial decisions you need to make together. If you both have Benjamin, he can help navigate those conversations as well.

Benjamin can help you integrate your financial life, even if your two financial situations aren't completely integrated. You can still combine your financial goals without necessarily having to get joint bank accounts, joint credit cards, and joint investments.

Even if you have some accounts combined and some separate, or you have separate credit cards, or if you have separate bank accounts for your discretionary spending money, Benjamin can help manage how those decisions fit into your combined financial situation. He can see everything and communicate how those individual accounts factor into the bigger picture of your joint financial plan. He can help you figure out your combined financial future, even if all of your finances aren't combined.

Of course, both you and your significant other have to agree to use Benjamin and to commit to letting him help you. If you do, Benjamin will give you a common language. You can both talk about money the same way.

It's all in the way that you present something. As opposed to one partner saying, "Hey, you can't spend money today," or "You shouldn't spend money," or, "You need to cut your shoe budget," or, "You need to stop ordering things on Amazon," the conversation can be, "Hey, let's both do this. Let's stick to this Daily Spend Limit that Benjamin has set for us." Now, both partners can check in about how they did with their Daily Spend Limit without asking, "What did you spend that money on?"

Nobody has to be the bad guy. You just have to listen to Benjamin. And Benjamin doesn't take sides. He can act as a mediator and guide you both to the best versions of yourselves that you can possibly be. He can help you do everything you want to do.

Benjamin provides the perspective that allows a couple to gain a shared view of their financial situation. If you have a full understanding of this shared financial situation, the conversation becomes much easier. You know how much you can spend, how much you can't spend, and exactly why. Benjamin provides a concrete thing to adhere to that doesn't come down on one person's side or the other.

Benjamin doesn't ask you to change as a person. He doesn't ask the free birds to become nerds, or the nerds to become free birds. Owning your joint finances means accommodating *both* lifestyles, and Benjamin provides tactics and practices to do that. Benjamin can alleviate the arguments, turning them into productive conversations that move both people forward and balance each one's desires: to save for the future *and* live for today.

Benjamin puts everybody on an equal playing field. He wants one thing and one thing only: to make both of you happy. The free bird can see a clear picture of what the Daily Spend Limit is helping him or her save for and can easily understand exactly where his or her savings are going. And the nerd can see how spending money and enjoying life for today can work in harmony with planning for the future.

Chapter Eight

How Experiential Spending Gets You What You Want, Not Just What You Need

Our life is the sum of our experiences, and the story of our life is only as interesting as the experiences we enjoy. Those are the things that drive us, the things that we remember. So why not create a budget tailored to creating the life that you want, built out of the experiences that you want?

Experiential saving is about helping people save for their life story and continuing to keep people motivated to save by giving them a reward that is more immediate than many of the financial goals we usually talk about. And with Benjamin, the act of saving for your life story can actually help you build the longer-term financial habits that are needed to secure your financial future.

The American Dream has shifted. For the previous generation, it was all about owning the nicest car and the newest appliances—in other words, the best stuff. Our parents valued these things, because often their parents did not have them. Our generation has largely grown up with exposure to these amenities, so our priorities have shifted. Today, most people value experiences over things.

Millennials believe saving for a home and saving for experiences are of similar importance. While they are worried about paying off debt, millennials don't hold back on spending when it comes to experiences. Although they tend to make under $100,000 a year, they spend on experiences like those of older generations who make more than $100,000, averaging between $1,000 and $3,000 per year on vacation.

We are shifting as a culture to desire more experiences, because experiences make us who we are. Who we are as individuals is molded by the experiences we have: the things we see, the stories we hear, the food we eat, and the people with whom we share those experiences. You are the person you are because of the experiences you went through growing up. It determines what type of person you are, what you value, what motivates you. And you continue to grow and evolve as a person because of the experiences you have throughout your life.

Our experiences are what we talk about in conversations—the good ones and the bad ones. We don't talk about our things. Nobody cares about the coolest thing you bought. The stories people want to hear are about the experiences you've had. Even though it is easier to compare material things, when we are given a medium for self-expression, like social media, we tend to relate stories about experiences rather than things. More than 90 percent of our survey respondents said that their friends share experiences, not things, on social media.

Experiences are what make for a rich life, not how much stuff you have. In general, buying things does no good. It doesn't help you remember or build your life story. So often we buy cool things, thinking we're going to use them all the time. Recently, I saved up and bought this cool new toy that is basically a portable golf version of Cornhole. You can bring it wherever you want and play a little golf whenever you'd like. It was on back order, so I had to wait a couple months to get it. I was so excited!

Well, guess what? It finally arrived . . . and I didn't play with it once.

So often, we buy something that we think will bring us lasting enjoyment, and then we use it maybe a few times and never again. This is because it is not *things* that bring lasting enjoyment, but rather the experiences we have and remember.

You probably don't remember what you got for your birthday fifteen years ago. But if you took a trip to Alaska fifteen years ago and saw glaciers and wildlife and sights you've never seen before, I bet you remember that.

Compare that to a bracelet or shoes or a watch. Try to remember when or where you bought that piece of jewelry or that pair of shoes, or the exact trip when you bought that thing from Target, or the exact time you clicked on that "buy now" button on Amazon. Unless it was very recently, you probably don't remember. Now, try to remember those trips you have taken and those experiences you've enjoyed. You probably remember them much more clearly.

In our survey, 33.5 percent of people said they had no idea what the "coolest" thing they bought two years ago was, versus the 30 percent of people who remembered it like it was yesterday. After five years, 44 percent of people said they couldn't recall the "coolest" thing they bought, versus the 17.5 percent of people who clearly remembered it. And, after ten years, 51.2 percent of people had no clue what the "coolest" thing they bought was, versus the 19 percent of people who were able to clearly recall it.

We also asked people about how well they remembered the "coolest" experiences they'd had. Two years on, 15 percent of people had no idea what that experience entailed, versus the 49 percent of people who remembered it like yesterday. Five years down the road, 18 percent of people couldn't recall it, versus the 35 percent of people who remembered it in detail. And, ten years on, 24 percent of people were at a loss when asked to describe that experience, while 33 percent of people were able to clearly recall it.

The percentage of people who remember is completely flipped when you move from things to experiences. The takeaway from these results is simple: you don't remember the things you buy, no matter how cool they are, but you do remember experiences.

When presented with the choice between saving for experiences and saving for things, the percentage of people in our survey who chose saving for experiences was nearly double the percentage of people who chose saving for things. They didn't care about the bracelet; they wanted the trip to Miami. They didn't want the wine cellar; they wanted the Italian vacation instead.

The things that people do value, they value because of the experiences those things afford. A bracelet doesn't create an experience. A fancy meal, however, can certainly be an experience. Perhaps you value your fancy television because it lets you invite everybody over to watch the Super Bowl or the new *Game of Thrones* episode. The reason people want to own a house is because it is a place you can create the experiences of your life.

The gadgets that people value are the ones that help them create experiences. We don't value technology because it's a cool thing; we value it because it gives us cool experiences. One of the few things that people valued over an experience was a Tesla. This puzzled me; why a Tesla? And then I realized it is because driving a Tesla is an experience in itself and driving one day in and day out creates experiences and memories that will stay with you. That piece of technology makes it fun to do that everyday experience—driving. It's a daily experience that, with this piece of technology, becomes a *super cool* daily experience.

Smartphones are another perfect example, and one that more people have experience with than a Tesla! A smartphone is an experiential piece of technology. Smartphones help us to create, document, share, and remember our experiences, so we value them as well.

These gadgets integrate into our life seamlessly and facilitate desirable times, memories, and experiences. We like gadgets that help create more experiences for us. And that's what Benjamin does. He seamlessly integrates into your life and helps bring about more memories and experiences. Benjamin joins you in creating the experiences that build your life, making them better and more frequent. He is a piece of technology that enables you to enjoy more, experience more, and worry less.

So many budgets only factor in what you need, the bare bones required to survive. Everything else, you're supposed to save for later. This is exactly what demotivates people from sticking to a budget. People want to do good for society, for their family, and for themselves—not just in the long term, but *today*. A traditional budget doesn't really help you do any of that, so it's hard to commit to.

Financial "experts" wonder why people aren't saving, but the answer is simple: it's because they're telling people not only to refrain from buying things, but also to avoid spending money on experiences. People don't like budgets because they get in the way of having experiences. So they just live their lives, having the experiences they want to have, and later in life, they find themselves in trouble because they haven't saved.

You can tell people over and over to save for retirement, but it may fall on deaf ears unless you can help them relate to it better. It's hard to convince ourselves to save for retirement. *It's so far away,* we think. *Things will work themselves out.* It's natural psychology. Despite being told that the earlier you start saving for retirement, the earlier you can retire, according to our survey, saving for retirement falls to the third priority of individuals aged eighteen to thirty-four. This is substantially behind saving for experiences, which ranks number one, and saving for a house, which is number two.

This is not because younger people don't believe the advice that is being told to them. It's because they can't comprehend it. Among those aged forty-five to fifty-four, saving for retirement is clearly the priority. Then comes experiences, followed by buying a house. This isn't because of maturity or anything of that nature; it's because it becomes easier to comprehend when you are saving for something that is eight to sixteen years away when you are forty-five to fifty-four. It's less than half a lifetime away. You can remember what eight to sixteen years feels like.

When retirement is so far away, as it is for eighteen- to thirty-four-year-olds, it's hard to wrap your mind around it. Buying a house is understandable. It's closer in time, so it's something we can get behind. Experiences are also shorter-term savings, which are not only easier to wrap our heads around, they are also more immediately enjoyable and gratifying. So, naturally, younger people tend to rank experiences and buying a house over far-off retirement. It's psychology. That is how our brains work.

Fighting against human nature and human psychology is a losing battle. So why not work *with* human nature and human psychology? Rather than the same old budgeting techniques that we try over and over again—the techniques that just aren't working—why don't we employ a budgeting technique that lets you see the benefits of saving money now?

The conversation needs to be changed to allow people to still cultivate experiences to build their lives and themselves while also maintaining a budget that is effective for today and positions them well for the future. There is a way to relate to people better, to stimulate and engage people more, to help them develop self-control, instead of just saying, "Don't do anything."

According to our survey, only 42 percent of people who say they are worried about their financial situation take more than one vacation a year. Meanwhile, 70 percent of people who say they feel good about their financial situation take more than one vacation a year. In other words, people who feel better about their financial situation tend to take more vacations per year.

It makes sense that someone who is stressed about his or her financial situation won't feel able to take an extra vacation. However, planning and taking more vacations can actually help us relieve stress regarding our financial situation.

How? By saving for experiences that you can actually wrap your head around—like concerts, beach vacations, and trips to Europe—as opposed to something abstract like saving for retirement. These experiences make sense to us because we can visualize them, because we have seen people do them and experience them.

Retirement is tough to wrap our heads around, not only because it is so far away, but because we don't really see people sharing their retirement experiences. We see them sharing their traveling experiences, their food experiences, their entertainment experiences (whether those experiences are happening in retirement or not). It's hard to be committed to putting money toward something we can't even visualize. It's much easier to say, "Oh man, my friend took this trip to New Zealand. I want to go to New Zealand. I'm looking at all of his pictures, which are amazing. I'm going to start saving so that in a year, I can go to New Zealand, because, *man*, it looks so cool!"

To motivate yourself to save and create better spending habits, you have to entice yourself with the shorter-term reward of an experience.

Not only are these experiences easier to wrap your head around, but they also give you a sense of accomplishment. You proved to yourself that you can save for something, and then you got to enjoy it. People get stressed about their financial situation because they don't feel like they have the ability to save. They believe they aren't making any progress. By saving for experiences and accomplishing those saving goals, we get more motivated. We feel more accomplished—which ultimately reduces our overall stress—because we've proven to ourselves that we can do it.

It's the shiny-ball effect. Our instinct is to chase the shiny ball. And if a new shiny ball comes along, we go after that. Whatever we are working on or focusing on, we naturally get distracted if a shiny ball appears. And when we catch that shiny ball, we feel good. We feel accomplished, even if it wasn't the ball we were going after originally.

What if we could harness that natural instinct? What if we could make chasing the shiny ball a part of the plan? What if we could use the shiny-ball effect to create positive behavior?

The shiny-ball effect keeps you focused on the amazing experiences you are saving for in the short term. Benjamin helps you save for those experiences so you get more immediate gratification. Benjamin doesn't say, "Save for retirement. Don't go on a vacation." Or, "Save for retirement. Go on only one vacation a year." He says, "Save for retirement and go on vacation; in fact, go on *two* vacations. Just change your spending habits in X, Y, or Z way to accomplish that, while also securing your future."

Benjamin actually encourages you to save for experiences because he knows you already have the fundamentals covered.

In the background, Benjamin is positioning you to achieve all these longer-term financial goals. Thanks to the technology of Benjamin, you continue to save for the core financial goals that are necessary for a solid financial foundation while bringing those experiences to the forefront and focusing on them instead of the distant future.

Benjamin sets up all your core expenses, including your Daily Spend Limit for your day-to-day life. He makes sure you're paying down your debt and saving for retirement. All of that foundational stuff is covered, so now you can focus on saving for the experiences you want to have. You can add in that shiny ball.

Of course, spending money on an experience can still be stressful. *Is it going to be worth it?* we wonder. *Am I going to enjoy myself to the fullest extent possible to make it worth the money I spent on it?* With Benjamin, by the time you're on the trip, you've already paid yourself back for any money you spent. So you can relax and enjoy the experience knowing that the money is all accounted for.

Most people like to splurge when they go on vacation. When we're at home, we pay attention, try to keep costs down, and don't order the most expensive thing on the menu. When we're on vacation, we go into vacation mode. We want to go to the nicest restaurants and enjoy the finest wines. We don't care how much money we spend because, hey, we're on vacation!

With Benjamin, you don't have to worry about splurging because you've prepaid for all of it. So it feels like a free trip! Moreover, no matter what you spend on the trip, when you come back home, your Daily Spend Limit will adjust to help you pay back any overage. Benjamin will help you navigate how to recover from your vacation splurge.

Benjamin takes the pressure off your experiences. You know that you're going to spend a bunch of money, but you can rest assured that Benjamin will help you even it out. Of course, it's not a magic bullet. You can't take trips every other week and splurge all the time! In order for this to work, you have to be committed to Benjamin. If you splurge like crazy on your trip, you are going to have to make sacrifices when you get home. Getting your financial situation back on track could take some time. But no matter how long it takes, Benjamin makes it all easier.

But when you take that vacation you've been planning for and looking forward to, you don't have to stress out about money. You don't have to stop three days into the trip and say, "I've already blown through my whole vacation budget. I need to pull back for the rest of the trip." You don't have to feel guilty about what you spend. You can just enjoy it.

Benjamin doesn't get mad at you for spending money on experiences. He doesn't judge you. He just helps you build back the money, both before and after, so that you can really live your life to the fullest. Rather than limiting you, Benjamin actually furthers your ability to enjoy your experiences.

Moreover, focusing on your experiences can actually help curb your spending. You'll be more inclined to curb your spending to meet your Daily Spend Limit—or even to stay below it—because you know it is going to result in this amazing experience you have planned.

Everybody rightfully advocates automatic savings, but only for the distant future. We need to encourage automatic savings for upcoming experiences as well. When you set up automatic savings for an upcoming experience, you can feel the closeness of the desired outcome. That will stimulate your brain and make it much easier to stick to than telling yourself, "Hey, just automatically put money into a savings account, and you'll never see it again."

It's hard to keep in line if all you've got to motivate you are those far-off, boring foundational goals. Benjamin motivates you to stick to your Daily Spend Limit because you really want the experience. Focusing on the upcoming awesome experience you are going to have encourages you to remember your Daily Spend Limit, and, of course, the experience is more likely to happen if you abide by that Daily Spend Limit.

Meanwhile, sticking to your Daily Spend Limit also means that you are ensuring all of those core foundational goals at the same time: your core living expenses, your savings for retirement, your emergency reserve, and paying off your debt. While you're focused on saving for that awesome experience, Benjamin is working on all of that in the background.

Owning your finances means being able to save for all of these things all at once, and Benjamin helps you do that. You can save for a house, save for experiences, and save for retirement. One doesn't cancel out any of the others. Saving for experiences isn't taken out of your core foundational goals or your core expenses. It's taken out of your Daily Spend Limit. When you put in an experiential savings goal, Benjamin estimates how much that experience will cost. Then you decide when you want to have that experience, and Benjamin builds in what that would look like in terms of your Daily Spend Limit. If Benjamin's estimate of what the experience will cost is off, you can adjust it. If the initial time frame takes too much out of your Daily Spend Limit, you can adjust it to determine what makes the most sense for you.

You also have some control over those foundational goals as well. You can say, "You know what, I'm willing to retire at 65 instead of 63 in order to go to New Zealand next spring." Benjamin can see how every single element is interconnected, so you can make adjustments to any element and view how it plays out across your entire financial situation. Instead of your having to personally calculate that you need to save $40 for this and $50 for that, Benjamin does all those calculations for you and provides you with your Daily Spend Limit.

Of course, the more things you save for, the lower your Daily Spend Limit will become. But if you are willing to spend a little less today, you can not only save for the distant future, you can save for the experiences that will make your life exciting, joyful, and fulfilling.

Moreover, with Benjamin, you can actually create good saving and spending habits based on outcomes that are desirable to you—and having those shorter-term experiential goals is part of creating those habits. I know that the idea of being physically healthy when I am seventy-five does not help motivate me to go to the gym today. But if I know I have an awesome trip coming up in six months on which I'm going to be doing some cool, physically challenging activities, well then, you bet I'm going to hit the gym! I want to take full advantage of that experience!

And here's the secret: If I go to the gym for those six months, I'll start to create a habit for myself. Then, once it becomes a habit, it will be much easier for me to continue doing, even after my awesome trip.

You can do the same thing with a budget.

When you put an experiential savings goal into Benjamin, he will calculate how much to reduce your Daily Spend Limit. Let's say that your Daily Spend Limit is reduced by $40 a week for the next six months to save up for your upcoming vacation. For those four months, you live your day-to-day life with your reduced Daily Spend Limit, saving that $40 a week toward your vacation. Finally, the six months are up. You take your vacation. You have an amazing experience.

But guess what? There's an added bonus. After six months of saving, you've grown used to your reduced Daily Spend Limit. You've gotten into the habit of saving that $40 a week. In fact, you don't even notice it anymore. So why not continue? Why not start putting that $40 a week toward another experience, or toward your longer-term or foundational goals, like paying off debt, or buying a house, or saving for retirement? That $40 a week can continue building up, contributing to your growing net worth over time.

With Benjamin, you can create the habits that allow you to secure your future, but you don't have to wait forty years to see the benefits of saving your money. Because what good is sticking to a budget if you're not living your life? Congratulations; you're out of debt. But you spent the last twelve years of your life sitting around doing absolutely nothing. Is that really worth it? Life is too short for us to waste that period of time. Without experiences, you're not living; you're just existing.

It's much easier to stick to a motivational budget, an aspirational budget, rather than a limiting budget. With Benjamin, you have a budget that allows you to look forward to things instead of being sad about the things you can't have. Rather than seeing your friends' posts about their amazing experiences and feeling sad, thinking, "I could never afford to do that," your friends' experiences can inspire and motivate you.

Benjamin engages you by focusing on building your life story. Owning your finances means experiencing life while also positioning yourself for your financial future. Life is the sum of experiences, so why not work with a budget—and a tool—that will allow you to experience the things you really want?

Chapter Nine

How to Stop Having Too Much Month at the End of the Money

Everybody tends to spend money the moment it comes in. So we spend the most when we get paid . . . and then try to make it to the next paycheck. For many of us, the days or even the week approaching payday, we're on pins and needles, just trying to get by. Then we get our paycheck, and the first thing we do is go out and splurge that weekend. The next thing we know, we're back in the same position: waiting on pins and needles for our next check. This is a classic symptom of renting your finances: using all of your resources early on, enjoying yourself, and then trying to figure things out later in the month, when you're already in trouble.

A study was done on this phenomenon using bowling. In the study, people were told that they would earn a dollar for every bowling pin they hit with a bowling ball. They gave the study participants twenty balls to roll over the course of ten frames. You could roll as many balls as you wanted during each frame.

The study found that people would use up all of their balls on the early frames. If they knocked down four pins with the first ball on the first frame and used a second ball to knock down four more pins, they would then use a third ball to knock down the last two pins. This would continue until the seventh or eighth frame, when they had already used up all twenty of their balls and had none left for the final frames. They would end up leaving twenty dollars on the table because they would have no bowling balls left by the final two frames.

The math seems like it should be easy: use two balls on each frame to maximize the number of pins you can hit. And yet even when people knew that there were more frames to come, they would use up all their bowling balls on the earlier frames, attempting to get all those early pins down instead of saving bowling balls to get even more pins on the later frames.

This study shows that people will tend to use up all their resources early on. It's the same way we use toothpaste or paper towels. We use both very generously early on because we have so much at our disposal. But then we keep that tube of toothpaste for a long time, trying to squeeze out just a little bit more so we don't have to go to the drugstore to buy another tube. We will do just about anything to make that stuff last until the end. We will reuse paper towels just so we don't have to go buy some more.

We are not good at planning out the utilization of our resources for the future, even in a simple situation like the bowling-pin study. So imagine how much harder it is when it comes to budgeting and the intricacies of planning our spending for the month ahead.

The bowling pin-theory encompasses the psychological burden that we all face when we get paid. When we get paid, we feel a wealth effect. The wealth effect makes us feel much better off than we really are. We feel like now is the time to go and buy whatever it is we've been wanting while we have this money in our pocket. We are less cautious about our spending decisions. We'll go out and splurge on lunch, have an extra drink or two, *and* buy that pair of shoes, because we feel much wealthier.

This isn't just a problem when going from paycheck to paycheck. It's also part of why traditional budgeting so often fails. With traditional budgeting, we give ourselves a limit in various categories—food, entertainment, etc. At the beginning of the month, we feel like we will never reach those limits. We spend freely in all those categories. Then, the next thing we know, we're halfway through the month and we've already reached our limits. We blew our way through $325 of our $400 entertainment budget because we felt like we had all the money in the world.

It's natural. We get our paycheck and we look at our bank account, or we look at our budget for the month, and we think, "Oh yeah, I'm rolling in it! I've got so much money to spend!" It doesn't make us a bad person. It's just human nature. We're not thinking about the fact that some of that money has to go to our rent, some if it has to go to our bills, some of it has to go to groceries, car insurance, gas money, health insurance . . .

We don't think about it because we don't want to analyze our situation. We don't want to dig deep into the numbers. We don't want to calculate what we have to set aside for this and that. Our brains don't naturally do that math. So we go by what we feel. And when we get that paycheck, we feel rich, and we spend that money.

It ends up being first in, first out: whatever comes in goes straight out, and when we're left to pay our bills at the end of the month, we realize we're screwed. Never mind making payments toward our credit card debt, or putting money toward saving for a house, or putting money toward retirement . . .

Even if we are good about setting aside all those monthly bills and expenses, the problem usually comes down to that discretionary spending money—the money we're going to use to buy lunch or go out with friends. We get our paycheck, we set aside our monthly expenses, and then we think, "All right, I've got all this money for fun!" And then we spend it all right away, and halfway through the month, we can't do anything at all. No social life for us until the next paycheck comes in. We just have to sit at home doing nothing but being a hermit.

What would happen if we had some kind of normalizer—something that would keep us from overusing in the beginning, allowing us to use the same amount, in the same way, during the last days as we would in the first? We could be warned earlier in the process that our toothpaste usage is getting out of hand, and we could slow it down so that we have enough toothpaste for the entire month.

How do we normalize our spending so that we can stay within our means every single day, so that we don't run out of money at the end of the month? *With Benjamin and the Daily Spend Limit.* Benjamin normalizes your spending over a longer period of time. He makes sure you can spend money every day throughout the whole month, as opposed to only spending in the first week after you get your paycheck, or blowing your whole monthly budget up front, and then having to spend nothing for the rest of the month.

People think the only way they can have the instant gratification that we all naturally crave as human beings is to spend and splurge right away. We don't think about the fact that we could be instantly gratified more often if we spread out our spending. With Benjamin, you can space out your spending so that you can do fun things all month long, not just right after you get your paycheck. Wouldn't you rather be able to have fun experiences all month?

In all likelihood, if you were told that you could only spend $150 at one particular event, you could still have the same good time that you did when you spent $325 of your "entertainment budget." And now you have the ability to have even *more* experiences during the month to build into your life book.

Maybe this month you end up spending more on food than on entertainment. You don't have to worry about the fact that you blew through your food budget while you didn't really use your entertainment budget. Benjamin doesn't care. He evens that out, so no matter what you spend your money on, it still all levels out over the course of the month.

Benjamin actually lets you have more experiences over the course of the month. He lets you do more, spend more, and enjoy more over the course of a month because he prevents you from blowing all your money as soon as you get your paycheck or right at the beginning of your monthly budget. Benjamin doesn't limit what you can do; he *expands* what you can do.

Benjamin helps you manage your decisions to help you build the best life book you can by looking at what you want to do in the immediate future, in the near future, and in the far future. He ensures that you can provide for the experiences you want today, the experiences you want to have down the road, and the experiences you haven't even imagined.

Our brains have trouble placing ourselves into the future and anticipating what we will feel like two weeks from now. It's hard to comprehend where we are going to be and what we are going to want to do with our money, so we just spend it right away.

We believe we should be able to think through to the end of the month, but when we're dealing with day-to-day spending in the moment, it's hard to think all the way through to three weeks from now. It's hard to calculate, "Well, am I going to want to go out with my friends that Wednesday night, three weeks from now? How much do I need to save to be able to do that?" Nobody can do that math on the fly when he or she is deciding what to spend each moment of each day.

We don't know how to plan for how much we want to save at the end of the month. We just see the money in our account and spend it, and then when we get to the end of the month, we think, "Oh shoot, I wanted to save $400 into my Roth. Oh well, I'll do it next time."

It's a cycle. Every month, people spend all their money in the first half of the month. Then they spend the last week trying to scrape by, totally down to the wire. Then their paycheck pops up in their bank account and they do the same thing over again. Then, all of a sudden, they're forty-five years old and they haven't saved anything for retirement.

This is why everyone preaches automatic savings. And I agree! But Benjamin can help you integrate automatic savings into your monthly spending in a sustainable way that allows you to continue spending today. Even if you don't have automatic savings, Benjamin can send you a reminder. "Hey, it's the second of the month," he can say. "Time to move that $300 to your retirement account."

Benjamin normalizes your spending so that you have money every day for the whole month and you are still saving for the future. Once again, normalization is something we do naturally. We know that if we have a blowout weekend, we should probably take it easy over the next couple days. But normalizing that over a whole month, or a whole pay period, is more difficult.

Some days you feel richer than others. You may think, *I haven't really spent any money in three days, so I have plenty of money to spend today!* But do you really? Do you know what you have coming up later in the week? Do you know what recurring expenses are going to come out of your bank account? You're not really thinking about the fact that you want to go out next weekend. You just think, *The past three days, I did really well, so I'm going to splurge, and then I'll try to figure out how to make it up tomorrow.*

Or, you think, *OK, I'll be really good this month, and then at the end of the month, I'll buy that TV.* But you don't really know how it's going to turn out. You don't really know how much you are going to spend over the course of that month.

With Benjamin, if you really want to save for that TV, you can put it in as a goal. Then Benjamin will tell you exactly how much you can spend that month and be able to buy the TV at the end of it, while still covering your core expenses and saving for the future.

No matter what you want to do, Benjamin can help you figure out whether or not it's feasible, and, if it is, how to get it done. Benjamin may say, "Hey, your Daily Spend Limit is $10 for the next month," but that's because you have a lot of ambitious upcoming goals planned. Benjamin is going to help you meet those goals. And if you realize you can't stick to that plan, Benjamin is going to help you assess and adjust.

Benjamin can help you do more by helping you stay true to a process that plans out and normalizes your spending. Benjamin wants to give you ownership. He wants to give you the tools to normalize your spending over a period of time so that you always have money at the end of the month. Benjamin helps you do the planning ahead of time rather than just flying by the seat of your pants every month. Benjamin gives you all the knowledge ahead of time instead of when a crisis hits.

Of course, sometimes crises do hit. As always, life is the thing that gets in the way of our monthly plan. We may be doing really well with our monthly spending. Then, all of a sudden, we get last-minute information about a can't-miss event, and we need to buy a ticket then and there; otherwise, we'll miss it. Or an unexpected family crisis arises, and we have to fly to join our family to deal with it. And, all of a sudden, our monthly budget is blown. Our paycheck is spent. We are screwed for whatever else we are supposed to pay that month.

When people spend money—whether it's on a life event or a trip or a weekend splurge or an impulse purchase—they always think, *I'll make up for it. I'll pay myself back.* But more often, despite their best intentions, paying themselves back ends up falling by the wayside as their focus shifts to their more immediate concerns and expenses. And that money they spent ends up eating into their emergency reserves, or their retirement savings, or wherever else they had intended for the money to go.

Benjamin makes sure that doesn't happen. He takes those last-minute opportunities or life events in stride and helps you spread the cost out, normalizing your spending through the Daily Spend Limit so that you can still afford to pay all your bills, hit your foundational goals, and still have money for day-to-day life throughout the month. Perhaps your Daily Spend Limit will be dramatically reduced, but Benjamin will make sure that you still make it to the end of the month without entering crisis mode.

The same goes for those inevitable impulse purchases. If we really, really want something, chances are, we're going to buy it. And chances are also we're going to buy it when we feel like we can afford it: at the beginning of the month, when we've just gotten our paycheck and we're feeling flush with money. We see that money in our account and we think, *To hell with it. I really want this thing. I have the money, so I'm going to buy it right now.*

The great thing about Benjamin is that he's able to roll with that impulsive, instant-gratification purchase. He can factor it into your monthly spending and adjust your Daily Spend Limit to accommodate it.

Benjamin helps you prepare for both the expenses you know are coming up and the ones you don't know about. Whether it's a sudden problem, or a last-minute opportunity that you have to seize, or an impulse purchase, Benjamin's got your back.

And if you make a mistake, that's OK. Benjamin will adjust to help you figure out how to cover it and get back on track while still being able to spend money during the month so that you don't have to be a hermit until your next paycheck comes in. He'll also let you know how you can do better with your next paycheck so you don't go down the same road again.

Of course, you may be in a situation where the amount you make every month just covers your core expenses and your core foundational goals. And yes, I readily admit, that's a tough situation to be in. But Benjamin can help you analyze every aspect of your situation, and help you see where you might be able to cut back without debilitating results. Maybe you don't want to make changes to your cable plan, but Benjamin can show you that if you do—if you switch your plan and reduce your Comcast bill from $150 a month to $80 a month—you can have access to some more cash for your Daily Spend Limit. Or you can put that extra money toward a vacation in the future.

Benjamin can help you take a look at all your expenses to identify reasonable places to cut back. You may think, *OK, if I cancel my Hulu subscription, that will help.* But how much does it actually make a difference? Benjamin can do the analysis and help you figure it out. Perhaps cutting Hulu isn't the best option. Perhaps you should keep your Hulu subscription and cut your cable subscription instead. Benjamin can do the math on all your monthly expenses to see what makes the most sense in the bigger picture of your financial situation.

Benjamin gives you an awareness of all of your recurring expenses. You may well have subscriptions you've completely forgotten about. Maybe you signed up for a free trial of HBO to watch a certain program and forgot to cancel your subscription, and now you've been paying fifteen bucks a month without even realizing it. Benjamin can alert you to those forgotten expenses so you can save a bit of money every month. It may not seem like much, but if your Daily Spend Limit for the month is lower than you'd like, you can see what you can cut and how that will affect your Daily Spend Limit for the next month.

Now, some of you may be thinking, *I do that math! I budget for the month! I take into account all of my recurring expenses!* And many of us do. But do we do it all the time? Most of us tend to do it for a little while, and then we feel like we have everything under control and we stop.

The truth is, we don't have it under control because we don't have an easy, built-in process. We don't have cues that help us remember to think twice about making purchases and spending money when we get that paycheck.

We all want to make our money last all month, but we just don't know how to do it. We don't know how to figure it out. We know that spending all our money at once is not optimal, but the math is too complicated, so we figure we'll just spend what we feel like spending and work it out later. We get stressed out thinking about it, so we say, "Screw it; I'm not going to deal with it."

The key to having money at the end of the month is awareness and simplicity—and that comes from having everything integrated into one solution instead of having an overload of information with no holistic picture of our entire situation.

The solution is having one single, simple tool to use instead of having every single possible tool that we could possibly use on the table in front of us. Having fourteen different finance apps on our phone—having all these tools and all this information in front of us—is like taking an open-book test.

In school, we would all get so excited when we were told that a test would be open book. We would have all the information available to us; how much easier could it get? So we wouldn't take as much time to study and prep as we would for a regular test. Why would we need to? We'd have the textbook in front of us, right?

But then, there we'd be with our test of twenty-five questions and a five-hundred-page book in which to try to find the answers. How the heck is one supposed to find twenty-five individual pieces of information in a book containing five hundred pages? We start racing through the index, trying to search for the terms that are in the questions. Then we turn to every page containing those terms, trying to find the exact answer to the question. All of a sudden, we're spending all this time on each question, and before we know it, we've run out of time and haven't finished the test. Even though all the answers are there, with the whole textbook in front of us, we have so much information that we can't hone in on the actual information we need to answer the questions.

The same thing happens with our financial situation. We're presented with so much information that we can't find the answers to the questions we have. Between apps and articles and financial-advice blogs, we can't possibly sort through all of the information to determine the right answers for ourselves and our specific situations.

All the financial information and advice out there in the world is like the five-hundred-page textbook, and our financial situation is the test. We'll be much better off if we can hone in on what is specifically relevant to the test, rather than flip through the whole book, which includes a ton of information that is not relevant to us at all, looking for the answers we need or think we need.

It's kind of like WebMD. We go on WebMD, search for the symptoms we're experiencing, and then automatically assume that any possible illness that turns up is what we actually have. The same is true of our financial situation. We search for answers based on a broad set of variables, and then tie them back to either the worst-case scenario or our desired best-case scenario. But chances are—just like those WebMD diagnoses—that scenario has nothing to do with our actual financial situation!

People tend to flip through the whole textbook or search all the contents of WebMD. We look not only at our apps and accounts, but also articles, blogs, and various news headlines, and then we freak out about how the big news stories might affect our finances. It feels out of our control, and we grow stressed and feel paralyzed. We think we are being thorough, but we're actually just burying ourselves in information until we can't move. We actually start negatively impacting ourselves.

Stress causes inaction, and it's no wonder that we're stressed. There is so much going on, so much we have to do. We want to live life. We want to plan for the future. We want to take care of our kids and our health. The last thing we want to deal with is money. And when we look at money, we are completely overwhelmed by all the information coming at us from every angle.

The truth is, we don't have to worry about everything when it comes to our finances. We just have to worry about our specific situation. We don't have to be really great at everything all at once. We only ever do really well at something—whether it's a sport or an instrument or math or our finances—if we focus on it. If I want to become really good at soccer, I shouldn't spend my time playing tennis, baseball, and golf at the same time; I should focus on soccer. If we focus on too many different things, the result is diluted. We'll be OK at some of them, but not *really good* at any of them.

When it comes to our finances, we should focus on what really impacts us, as opposed to trying to learn everything about the financial world. Focus on one thing: the Daily Spend Limit. Get really good at learning and utilizing that basic tool, and it will provide a foundation for building the rest of your financial knowledge. Maybe at some point, you can graduate to formulating a Weekly Spend Limit, or a Monthly Spend Limit, or even a Quarterly Spend Limit. But you don't have to; you can just stick with the basic building block of the Daily Spend Limit.

If you have seventeen financial apps on your phone, you may think you've got everything covered. But if they're not actually talking to each other, if you can't actually create a comprehensive picture by using of all those pieces, if you can't actually use them in an efficient and effective manner, what good are they?

On some tests, students are allowed to refer to an index card rather than an entire textbook. They don't have to have every single piece of information memorized, but they do need to sort through and refine the material so that it fits on the card. Then they can reference it quickly and easily during the test instead of hunting through an entire book to locate answers. The information they need, specific to the test at hand, is at their fingertips.

Of course, some people try to cram as much information as possible onto that index card. They're proud of the fact that they managed to fit so much on one card, but in fact, they end up with basically the same problem as having an open book: so much information that it is nearly impossible to easily find what they need. However, if the index card is set up appropriately, if the information is distilled and focused on the correct information, then it can be an incredibly effective tool.

The same is true for our finances. We are so proud when we've managed to aggregate all of the information about our financial situation, when we've managed to categorize every single one of our transactions. But if all of that doesn't actually easily yield the answers and processes that we need, what's the good?

A tool is only any good if we can use it efficiently and effectively. If we have an index card containing an entire textbook's worth of information, can we actually use it effectively? Having a whole book on a notecard is probably not going to help us ace the test; and having seventeen different apps on our phone is not going to make us a financial success. We still have to prepare. We still have to work at it. We still have to put effort into it. And it's a lot easier to put that effort into one thing rather than seventeen things. We all know that time is valuable. Nobody has the time to sort through seventeen apps, just as nobody has time to sort through a whole textbook—or a whole textbook crammed onto an index card—during a test.

Moreover, we have to be truly engaged in the effort. If we're not engaged, we're not going to adopt managing our finances as a habit. We may stick to it for a few weeks, but it's hard to turn an activity into a habit if we're not truly engaged with the process, the product, or the solution. It's impossible to be completely engaged with seventeen different apps. You're too busy trying to coordinate between them all and understand how they all relate to one another. It's much easier to engage with one simple interface that includes everything, and which proactively engages with you.

Benjamin is like a properly used index card for the test of your financial situation. You can't hold everything in your arms at once; you'll just end up dropping it all. Instead, you have to focus on one simple central point. And that is what Benjamin provides: a simple, comprehensive, engaging central point to your financial situation.

Benjamin is going to help you get where you want to go, whether or not you like everything he has to tell you. If you have awareness of your situation and you stay true to the knowledge you gain from that awareness, you'll have the opportunity to actively work toward a better situation in the future.

Benjamin and the Daily Spend Limit give you the cues you need to make those day-to-day decisions that will bring you greater satisfaction in the long run. Owning your financial situation means that you are able to make each paycheck last through the entire two-week or one-month period, without having to make extreme cutbacks in spending during the last couple of days before you receive your next paycheck. Benjamin helps you keep your spending in line so that at the end of every month, you're always going to have excess money. It will continue to build up every month and help you save for all those core foundational goals.

Benjamin shows you how your monthly spending decisions fit into your overall financial plan. If you were to cut cable, what would that do for the trip to Italy you have planned later this year? What would it do for your retirement plan? Would it all add up to help you actually retire sooner? It might! Benjamin can tell you.

Benjamin helps you better understand how to position yourself in a future that you can't fully visualize or comprehend and motivates you to make the changes today that will ensure that future by giving you those instant-gratification wins on a day-to-day basis.

Chapter Ten

Benjamin Is Ready to Show You the Benjamins

If you've read this book, it's probably because other budgeting and financial-planning products, processes, and mechanisms haven't worked for you. You're looking for something that will actually make a difference in your life, something that will be a breath of fresh air when it comes to budgeting and your finances.

I hope that by now, I've convinced you that Benjamin can help you take that breath of fresh air. We're not hiding anything. We're not trying to sell you anything. We just want to make your life easier and your financial future better. And we believe Benjamin can do that.

That's why there is no subscription or fee to use Benjamin. Benjamin is completely free. All you have to do is download the app, and then get started on a journey toward owning your finances.

If you're ready to embark on that journey, you don't have to wait. You can start using Benjamin at any time. You don't have to wait for some magical moment when it will be the right time to change your financial habits and develop a financial plan. You can start right now.

Our ultimate vision is that Benjamin is everywhere. Benjamin is with you and able to help you make decisions right then and there. How much money can you spend on a new car? How does buying that car impact your goal to buy a house? How does it impact your credit score? If you go out for drinks tonight, how will that affect your plans for the weekend?

It's so simple that people often think they must be missing something or doing something wrong. But they're not. *It really is that simple.* A lot of math and algorithms and technology make up the back end, but on the user-facing end, it is beautifully simple.

You just need to open the app, navigate it, and talk to Benjamin for a few minutes every couple of days—and you're done. Your budget is taken care of. Planning for your goals is taken care of. Your core expenses are taken care of. Your credit card debt is managed, your retirement savings are accumulating, and your emergency reserve is being stocked. And you can still spend money today!

The first step is extremely simple: Download the Wela app, of which Benjamin is a part. The app will then prompt you to supply your information and link your accounts.

Linking your accounts is probably the biggest hurdle to overcome when first setting up Benjamin. There are tens of thousands of financial institutions across the country, and they have many different technologies and processes. Some are very involved and some are very antiquated. Some institutions don't allow their data to be shared. So aggregating all your accounts—especially if you have accounts at small, local institutions—can potentially be difficult.

But don't worry: if you encounter hurdles, our customer service team will do everything we can to make sure you can link as many accounts as possible so that you can make the best use of Benjamin. And in the unlikely event that we do encounter an account that we can't link, you can add the account manually, and our team will help you update your core expenses.

You may be nervous about having to enter your user name and password for all of your different banking accounts, investment accounts, and credit card accounts, but I want to assure you that we take security *extremely* seriously. Benjamin employs bank-level security to protect all your financial information.

Moreover, we don't store any of your credentials, so your identity is completely hidden. Benjamin has what's called "read-only access," which means that he is only able to read your transactions. So even if the impossible happened and someone hacked our system, the hacker would not be able to see your user name, your password, the passwords to any of your bank accounts, or any information that would allow him or her to access any of your finances.

Benjamin does take a little bit of time up front to get it all set up, but after that, it is easy to monitor and maintain. If you put in this time at the beginning to get Benjamin set up, you can then live your life and spend less time worrying about your budget. If you want some human guidance as you embark upon this new financial journey, to help you get Benjamin up and running, we can set up a phone call, videoconference, or web conference at Wela to get you started.

Once you enter all of your information and link all of your accounts, Benjamin will automatically set your four foundational goals—cash flow positivity, paying down credit card debt, emergency reserve, and retirement savings—based on an analysis of all of your accounts. You can then adjust those goals however you'd like. After setting those goals, you set all your other goals, from saving for a house, to putting aside money for your kids' college tuition, to planning upcoming vacations and experiences.

Once you finish setting Benjamin up, you don't have to wait. He starts the calculations and analysis immediately, giving you information and results right away. He provides you with a Daily Spend Limit from day one. Immediately, he is able to tell you where you spend the most money, analyze the transactions from all of your accounts, and create a comprehensive picture of your financial situation. As soon as you set up Benjamin, you'll start gaining insight into your day-to-day spending habits.

You may have to adjust some categories in the beginning. For instance, if you spend money on groceries and Benjamin categorizes it as a Daily Spend Limit expense, you'll want to recategorize it as a core expense. It is important to make these adjustments to be sure your Daily Spend Limit is calculated correctly. And, once again, if you want help with any of this, we have a whole team ready to help you get it all set up.

Once you have Benjamin up and running, he will be working for you constantly. He will consistently update you on your Daily Spend Limit, how you can improve in certain categories, and how you are progressing toward your goals. Every time you check the app, Benjamin will provide you with notifications. He may tell you about uncategorized transactions and help you categorize them to allow you to maintain control over how your finances are sorted. Benjamin will also send you push notifications to keep you updated, such as notifications about your Daily Spend Limit based on your spending. You can also check to see how you're doing at any time.

If you want to dig deep, you can. You can view all your transactions and see how Benjamin has broken everything down. If you know you want to cut spending but don't know how to do so, ask Benjamin. He can tell you where you are spending the most, identify your recurring expenses, and make sure that they're all things you actually need.

You can play around with all the aspects of your financial situation to explore different scenarios for your present and future financial life. "If I want to retire sooner, what does that mean for the trip to Florida I'm planning?" you can ask. "If I want to add another goal, what does that mean for my Daily Spend Limit?" You can see and engage with your finances, adjusting and tweaking them to see the outcome of any financial decision you might make. You can interact with any element and immediately see how any changes would play out across your Daily Spend Limit, your upcoming goals, and your long-term financial plans.

There's still work that goes into maintaining your financial situation, but Benjamin gives you the resources and the platform to make that work as simple and engaging as possible. You have the resources within Benjamin and in the team behind the scenes to answer any questions and help you understand anything that is unclear. You have an integrated solution that is able to speak to a whole team of problem solvers and then give you whatever granular personalized information you need.

At Wela, we have an entire team of people devoted to your financial success, to making you happy with your financial plan. We have tutorials, blog posts, and social media pages that present tips and tricks to help you use Benjamin to his fullest capacity. You can also schedule a time to speak with one of our advisors.

One of the beauties of Benjamin is that he has a whole behind-the-scenes team that is constantly working to improve him and make him the best he can be so that he can help you even more. We built this technology to make people's lives better. If we're not doing that, then we want to be told why, and we will work our tails off to fix it.

That means that we listen to your feedback. Encounter a problem? Let us know! Have an idea about how Benjamin could be even better? Tell us! Unlike many other companies, we really, really want to know what you think. When you send an email to our feedback account, it goes straight to our product team. The team then uses that information to improve Benjamin. When you use Benjamin, you have a seat at the table to help make Benjamin exactly the product you need to make your financial life the best it can be.

We value our users above all else. When you use Benjamin, we don't see you as just another number or anonymous user. We want *you* to be part of the Wela family and the Benjamin family. We want to relate to you as an individual so that we can help you make your unique, specific situation the best it can possibly be.

Benjamin is so easy right now, and he's only going to become easier and better as we continue to make improvements based on our users' feedback. Benjamin can interact with millions of people. As he does so, he learns more and more, which then makes the experience even better for each individual. The more people who engage with and provide insights for him, the better Benjamin becomes.

At Wela, our mission has always been to change the way financial advice is delivered. Benjamin is a piece of that puzzle. He is truly changing the way financial advice is delivered—and you can be a part of it. Don't miss the opportunity to participate in changing the landscape of financial planning. Become part of a community that is creating a world in which we all have the ability to live our lives to our full potential because we own our financial situation.

Being in charge of your finances, ensuring your financial life makes sense, and making the most of your life aren't just goals for rich people. They are goals for everybody. No matter what your background is, you can take control of your life. You don't have to rely on other people to do it for you.

Benjamin is awesome, but Benjamin is a means to an end. What we want is for you to be as successful as possible. We want to free you from the burden of worrying about your finances. We want you to create financial habits that will help you live better today and in the long term. We want you to control your finances rather than letting your finances control you. And we believe that Benjamin can help you do all of that.

It is possible to take control of your finances. It is possible to make your financial life better and easier. It is possible to live life today while planning for tomorrow. It is possible to move from renting your finances to owning your finances.

Why wait? Benjamin is ready. Are you?

Disclaimer

This book is provided to you as a resource for informational purposes only and should not be viewed as specific advice or recommendations. This information is being presented without consideration of the investment objectives, risk tolerance or financial circumstance of any specific investor and the information might not be applicable for all investors. Everyone's financial situation is different and no representation is made or intended regarding the specific results you may obtain from using any of the information or tools presented in the book or by using the app. The tools described in the book are provided to you as a guide. There is no guarantee that by utilizing the tools you will achieve financial success. This information is not intended to, and should not, form a primary basis for any financial or investment decision. Always consult with an appropriate professional about your specific personal financial situation.

YourWela (Wela) is a technology platform that provides educational tools, calculators, aggregation capabilities, Benjamin and access to Wela Strategies. Usage of the technology platform is free. Wela Strategies, Inc. is an investment advisor registered with the Securities and Exchange Commission. Registration with the Securities and Exchange Commission does not imply a certain level of skill or knowledge or that the Securities and Exchange Commission has approved, passed upon, or endorses Wela Strategies, Inc. in any way. Any reference in this book to advisory services or investing refers to services provided by Wela Strategies. Utilization of the tools on the Wela platform does not constitute an investment advisory relationship. A separate advisory agreement and fee arrangement must be entered to become an advisory client of Wela Strategies.

Made in the USA
Monee, IL
04 November 2026

67379939R00075